Little Acorn Books

Readiness Games
37 Folder Games For Letters

by Marilynn G. Barr

LAB20146P
Readiness Games
37 FOLDERGAMES FOR LETTERS
Preschool — Grade 1
(*Skills Focus: readiness skills, alphabet identification, matching uppercase and lowercase letters,
matching alphabet pictures to letters, recognizing beginning and ending sounds,
recognizing vowel, vowel sounds, and consonants, hands-on fine motor skills responses, following directions, fair play*)

by Marilynn G. Barr

Published by: Little Acorn Books™
Originally published by: Monday Morning Books, Inc.

Entire contents copyright © 2014 Little Acorn Books™

Little Acorn Books
PO Box 8787
Greensboro, NC 27419-0787

Promoting Early Skills for a Lifetime™

Little Acorn Books™
is an imprint of Little Acorn Associates, Inc.

http://www.littleacornbooks.com

Permission is hereby granted to reproduce student materials in this book for non-commercial individual or classroom use. *School-wide or system-wide use is expressly prohibited.

ISBN 978-1-937257-55-2

Printed in the United States of America

37 FolderGames for Letters

Contents

Introduction 4
Playing Directions
   General Directions 4
   Activity Use 4
   Trail Game Playing Directions........................... 5
   Match Board Playing Directions 6
   Dominoes Playing Directions 7
   Pocket Game Playing Directions....................... 8
   Lotto Playing Directions 9
   Clothespin Match-ups Playing Directions 10
   Clothespin Wheel Playing Directions 11
   Fill-ins Playing Directions 12
   Dot-to-Dot Playing Directions 13
   Color-by-Letter Playing Directions 14
   Concentration Playing Directions..................... 15

Letter Recognition
   Matching Pictures to Letters
      Jelly Bean Party.. 16
      Who's There? 21
      Alligator Tails 26
      Butterfly Dominoes 32
      Cookie Jar Lotto 36
   Matching Uppercase and Lowercase Letters
      Crayon Wheel 41
      Star Hoppers 45
      Leaping Lizards 51
      Peek-a-boo Bunnies 55
      Popcorn Dominoes 60

ABC Order
   Sequencing Letters
      Peas in Pods 64
      Topsy Turvy Top Hats 69
      Sailing, Sailing.. 74
      Excellent Elephant 80
      Amazing Alligator 84

Beginning Sound Letter Recognition
   Matching Pictures to Beginning Sound Letters
      Ice Cream Scoops Lotto 88
      Candy Apples 93
      Circus Peanut Dominoes............................. 98
      Bats in the Attic 102
      Puppy Paws 107

Ending Sound Letter Recognition
   Matching Pictures to Ending Sound Letters
      Follow the Rainbow 112
      Hearts and Flowers 117
      Squirrels and Nuts 123
      Party Lanterns Lotto 128
      Shells on the Shore 133

Differentiating Letters
      Stained Glass Butterfly 137
      The Queen's Quilt 141
      The King's Kite 145

Consonants
   Matching Uppercase and Lowercase Consonants
      Bumble Bee Boogie.................................... 149
      Clownfish Carnival 154
      Pigs in Blankets Lotto 158
      Funny Car Rally 163
      Peek-a-boo Pumpkins 168

Short Vowels
   Recognizing Short Vowels and Vowel Sounds
      Fancy Socks in a Box 173
      Vegetable Soup 178

Long Vowels
   Recognizing Long Vowels and Vowel Sounds
      Peek-a-boo Spiders 183
      Cookies and Milk 187

Folder Handles 192

Introduction

FolderGames for Letters presents activities to enrich early reading readiness skills for young learners in easy-to-make-and-use file folder set-ups. The folders can be used with individual children, small cooperative groups, in learning centers, or with families at home.

The activities in FolderGames for Letters help to reinforce pre-reading and beginning-reading learning in an enjoyable and stimulating format. The activities range from alphabet identification to matching uppercase and lowercase letters to recognizing vowels and consonants. A variety of hands-on responses, including placing objects, clipping on clothespins, and connecting the dots, keep the children actively engaged.

Each FolderGames activity includes the file folder layout and the activity to be duplicated, easy directions for assembly, and simple directions for use.

General Directions

Use sturdy colored file folders for the FolderGames folders. Duplicate the inside file folder set-up, the illustration for the folder cover, and any game pieces. Color all parts with felt pens, colored pencils, or crayons. Then trim and cut out. Glue the file folder set-up to the inside of the folder and the illustration to the outside front. Glue any loose patterns, such as markers or cards, onto oak tag for extra-sturdiness. Color and laminate. Cut out or trim as necessary to complete construction. Buttons or other small objects may be used for markers that are not provided. Glue a manila envelope with a clasp to the back of the filer folder for games that include loose parts. Some games, such as Star Hoppers, include non-matching cards. Non-matching cards challenge children to differentiate matches from non-matches. Patterns throughout the book can have multiple uses. For instance, make Concentration card decks using game card patterns.

Activity Use

Have the children take out any loose parts from the envelope and open the file folder on the work area. Instruct the children on how to play the game. Have the children replace any loose parts in the envelope after play. Store the folders in a file basket. Pages 5-15 provide additional information for particular activities.

Trail Game Playing Directions for
Jelly Bean Party • Leaping Lizards • Follow the Rainbow
Funny Car Rally • Vegetable Soup • Cookies and Milk

 Reproduce, cut out, and glue these directions to the back of each Trail Game folder.

Trail Game Playing Directions

Trail Games are designed for two to four players. Set up the game board on a table. Shuffle and place the game cards, face down, next to the game board. (Players may take turns shuffling game cards.) Each player, in turn, draws a card to determine where to move on the trail. Players place used cards in a discard pile. When all cards have been drawn, reshuffle the discard pile to continue playing. Play continues until each player reaches The End.

Match Board Playing Directions for
Candy Apples • Bats in the Attic • Fancy Socks in a Box
Topsy Turvy Top Hats • Who's There?

Reproduce, cut out, and glue these directions to the back of each Match Board folder.

Match Board Playing Directions

Match Boards are designed for one to two players. Each player chooses one half of the board to play. Set up a match board on a table. Shuffle and place the game cards, face down, in the center of the table. (Players may take turns shuffling game cards.) Each player, in turn, draws a card. If there is a match, the player identifies the match, then places the card on his or her board. If there is no match, the player places the card, face down, in a discard pile. Play continues until each player has placed a matching card on each space on his or her match board. Reshuffle cards if needed.

Dominoes Playing Directions for
Butterfly Dominoes • Popcorn Dominoes • Circus Peanut Dominoes

Reproduce, cut out, and glue these directions to the back of each Dominoes game folder. Dominoes can contain identical and mismatched pictures or letters.

Dominoes Playing Directions

Dominoes are designed for up to four players. Shuffle and deal five dominoes to each player, then place the remaining dominoes, face down, in the center of the table. Players hold their dominoes like playing cards and do not allow the other players to see their hands. The dealer begins the game by placing one of his or her dominoes, face up, on the table. The next player looks at his or her dominoes to see if there is a match. If there is a match, the player places the matching side of his or her domino next to the domino on the table. A match can be letter to picture, letter to letter, or picture to picture. If there is no match, the player draws a domino from the center of the table until he or she finds a match. Children can only play matching dominoes at the open ends of the domino structure. Play continues until no more matches can be made.

Pocket Game Playing Directions for

Peek-a-boo Bunnies • Squirrels and Nuts

Peek-a-boo Pumpkins • Peek-a-boo Spiders

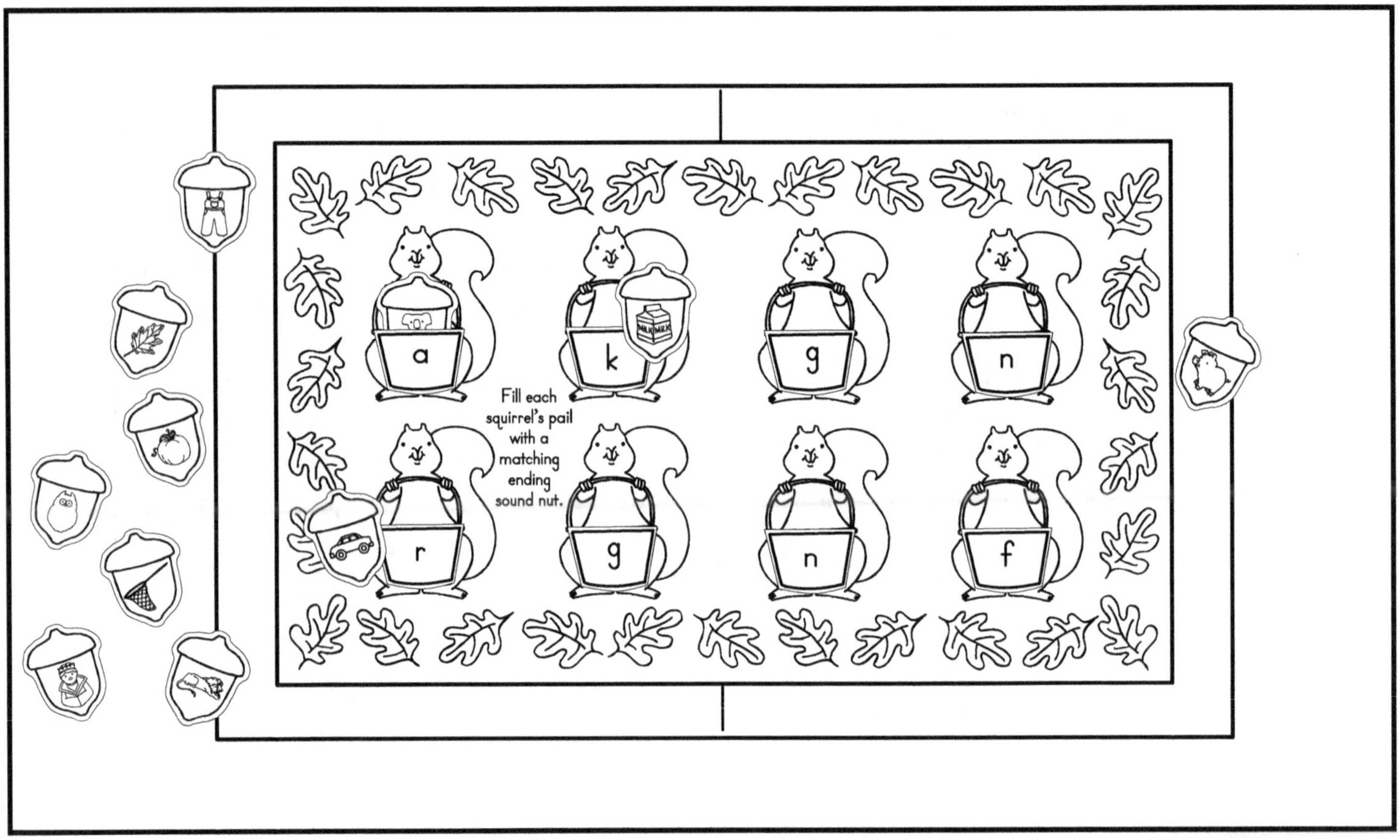

Reproduce, cut out, and glue these directions to the back of each Pocket Game folder.

Pocket Game Playing Directions

Pocket Games are designed for one to two players. Set up a pocket game folder on a table. Take out, shuffle, and place the game cards, face down, in the center of the table. (Players may take turns shuffling game cards.) Each player, in turn, draws a card. If there is a match, the player identifies the match, then slips the card into the correct pocket. If there is no match, the player places the card, face down, in a discard pile. Play continues until all the pockets are filled.

LAB20146P • 37 FOLDERGAMES FOR LETTERS • 978-1-937257-55-2 • © 2014 Little Acorn Books™

Lotto Playing Directions for
Cookie Jar Lotto • Ice Cream Scoops Lotto
Party Lanterns Lotto • Pigs in Blankets Lotto

 Reproduce, cut out, and glue these directions to the back of each Lotto game folder.

Lotto Playing Directions

Lotto games are designed for one to four players. Set up Lotto boards on a table. Shuffle and place the game cards, face down, in the center of the table, spread out or in a stack. (Players may take turns shuffling game cards.) Each player, in turn, draws a card. If there is a match, the player identifies the match, then places a token (or the card) on the matching space on his or her Lotto board. If there is no match, the player places the card, face down, in a discard pile. Play continues until each player has placed a token (or card) on each space on his or her Lotto board.

Clothespin Match-ups Playing Directions for
Alligator Tails • Hearts and Flowers • Bumble Bee Boogie

Reproduce, cut out, and glue these directions to the back of each Clothespin Match-ups folder.

Clothespin Match-ups Playing Directions

Clothespin Match-ups are designed for one or two players. Set up a game folder on a table. Take out and place the clothespins, face down, on the table. Each player, in turn, draws a clothespin. If there is a match, the player identifies the match, then clips the clothespin to the correct space on the game folder. If there is no match, the player places the clothespin back on the table. Play continues until each space on the game folder is clipped.

Clothespin Wheel Playing Directions for

Crayon Wheel • Puppy Paws

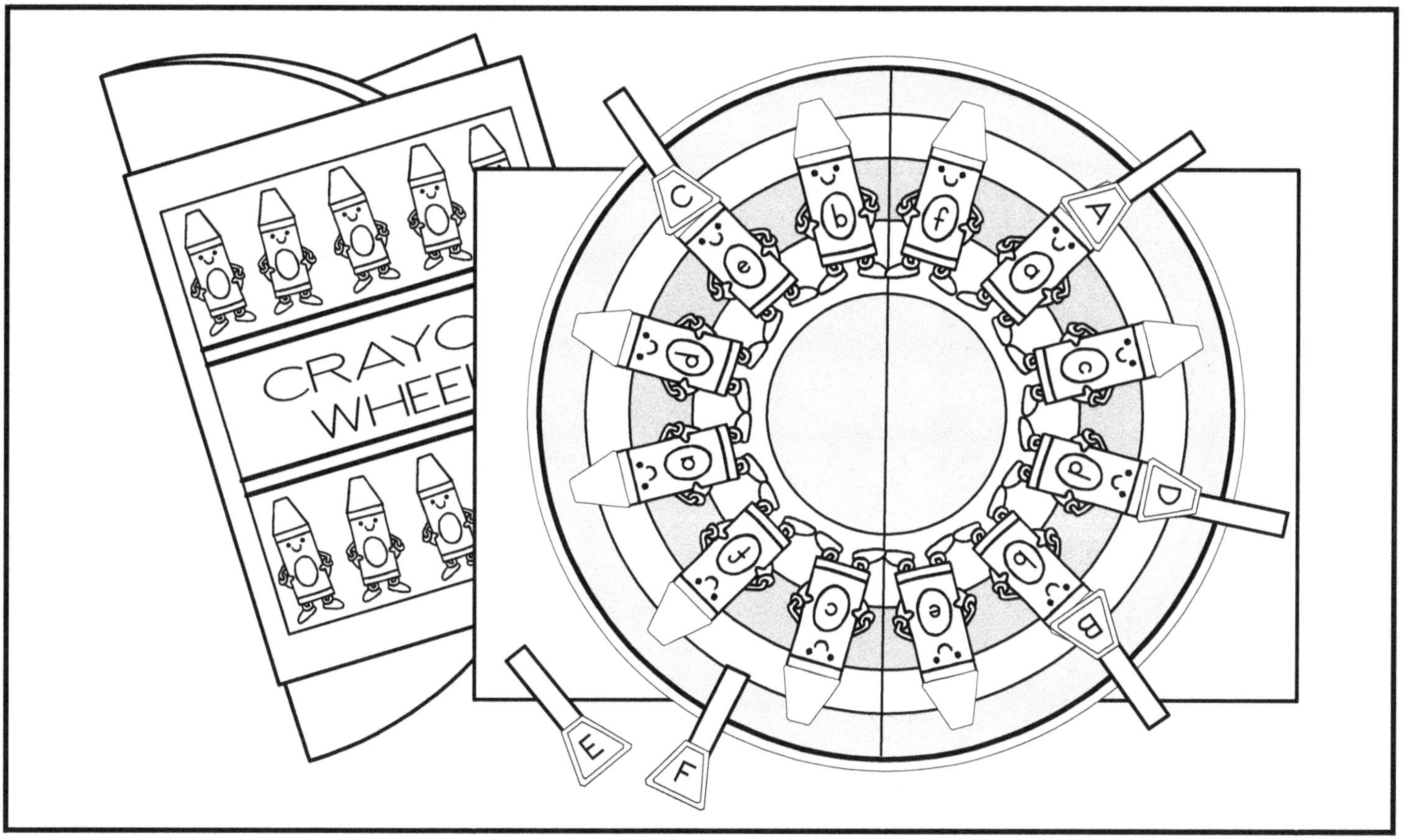

Reproduce, cut out, and glue these directions to the back of each Clothespin Wheel folder.

Clothespin Wheel Playing Directions

Clothespin Wheels are designed for one or two players. Set up a game wheel on a table. Take out and place the clothespins, face down, on the table. Each player, in turn, draws a clothespin. If there is a match, the player identifies the match, then clips the clothespin to the correct space on the wheel. If there is no match, the player places the clothespin back on the table. Play continues until each space on the wheel is clipped.

Fill-ins Playing Directions for
Peas in a Pod • Sailing, Sailing • Clownfish Carnival

Reproduce, cut out, and glue these directions to the back of each Fill-ins folder.

Fill-ins Playing Directions

Fill-ins are designed for individual play. Set up the game folder on a table. Read the directions on the game folder. Use a wipe-off crayon or marker to fill in the blanks. Have your work checked. Wipe off the folder with a soft rag or tissue when done.

Dot-to-Dot Playing Directions for
Excellent Elephant • Amazing Alligator

Reproduce, cut out, and glue these directions to the back of each Dot-to-Dot folder.

Dot-to-Dot Playing Directions

Dot-to-Dots are designed for individual play. Set up the game folder on a table. Read the directions on the game folder. Use a wipe-off crayon or marker to connect the dots. Wipe off the folder with a soft rag or tissue when done.

LAB20146P • 37 FOLDERGAMES FOR LETTERS • 978-1-937257-55-2 • © 2014 Little Acorn Books™

Color-by-Letter Playing Directions for
Stained Glass Butterfly • The Queen's Quilt • The King's Kite

Reproduce, cut out, and glue these directions to the back of each Color-by-Letter folder.

Color-by-Letter Playing Directions

Color-by-Letters are designed for individual play. Set up the game folder on a table. Read the directions on the game folder. Use a wipe-off crayon or marker to fill in the blanks. Have your work checked. Wipe off the folder with a soft rag or tissue when done.

Concentration Playing Directions for

Reproduce, cut out, and glue these directions to the back of each Card Game folder. Create card decks with the cards found throughout this book.

Playing Directions

Two to four players can play Concentration. Shuffle and place all the cards, face down, in the center of a table. Each player, in turn, turns over two cards. If the cards match, the player takes the cards and the next player takes a turn. If the cards do not match, the player turns each card over and the next player takes a turn. Play continues until all the cards are taken.

Jelly Bean Party
Matching Pictures to Letters A-F

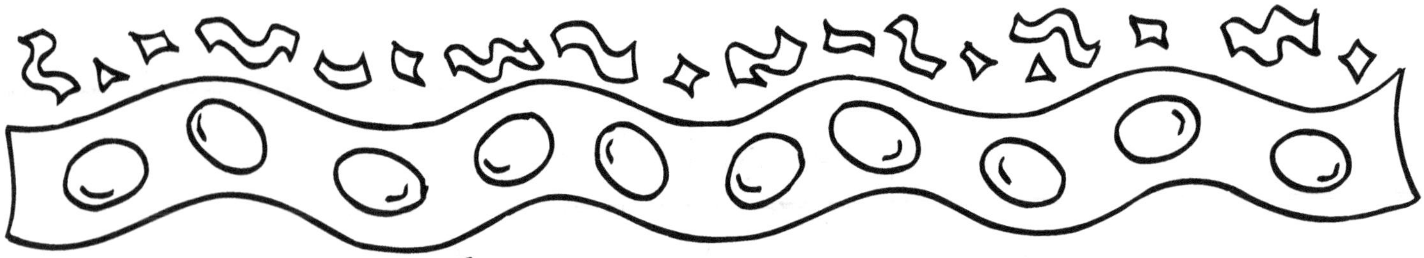

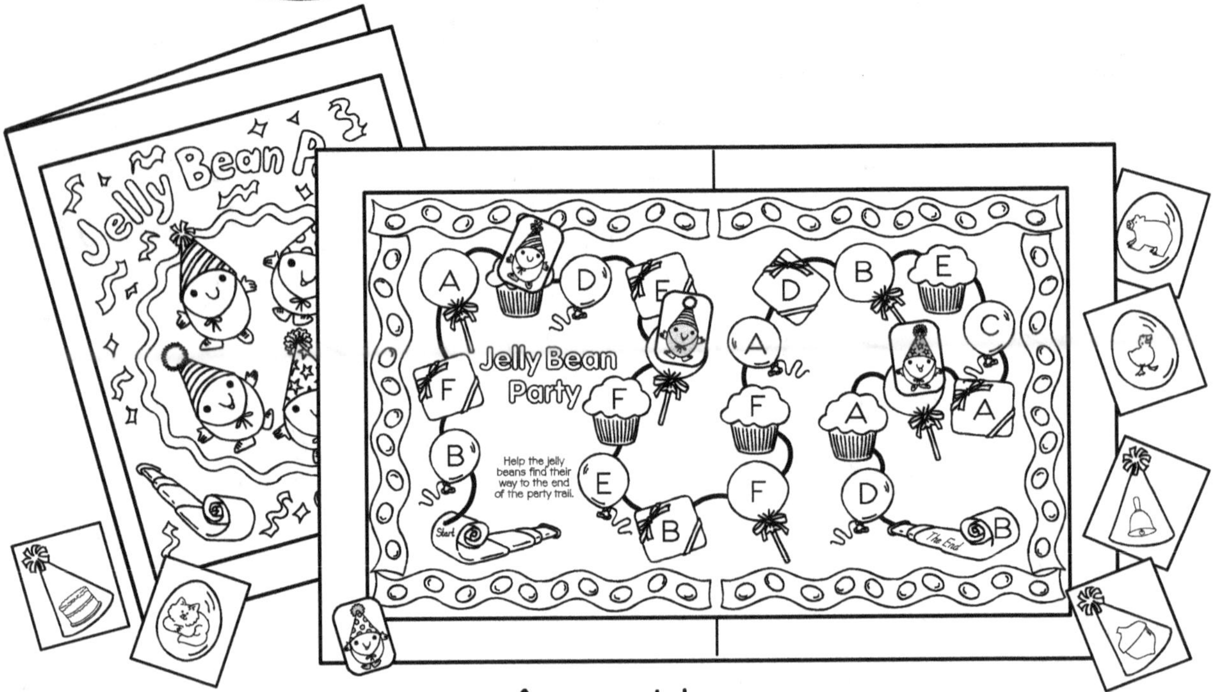

Trail Game

Assembly

Reproduce, cut out, and glue a set of oak tag handles (p. 192) to a standard-size file folder. Option: Decorate each handle with a copy of the jelly bean ribbon shown above. Reproduce, color, and cut out the "Jelly Bean Party" patterns. Matching in the center, glue the game board patterns to the inside of the folder. Glue the cover art to the front of the folder. Decorate the border around the game board, then laminate. Reproduce, color, laminate, then cut out the pawns and two sets of game cards. Glue an envelope to the back of the folder for pawn and game card storage. Option: Reproduce, cut out, and glue the Trail Game Playing Directions to the back of the folder.

Pawns

Jelly Bean Party Cover
Matching Pictures to Letters A-F

Trail Game

Jelly Bean Party
Matching Pictures to Letters A–F

Trail Game

Jelly Bean Party
Matching Pictures to Letters A-F

Trail Game

Jelly Bean Party
Matching Pictures to Letters A-F

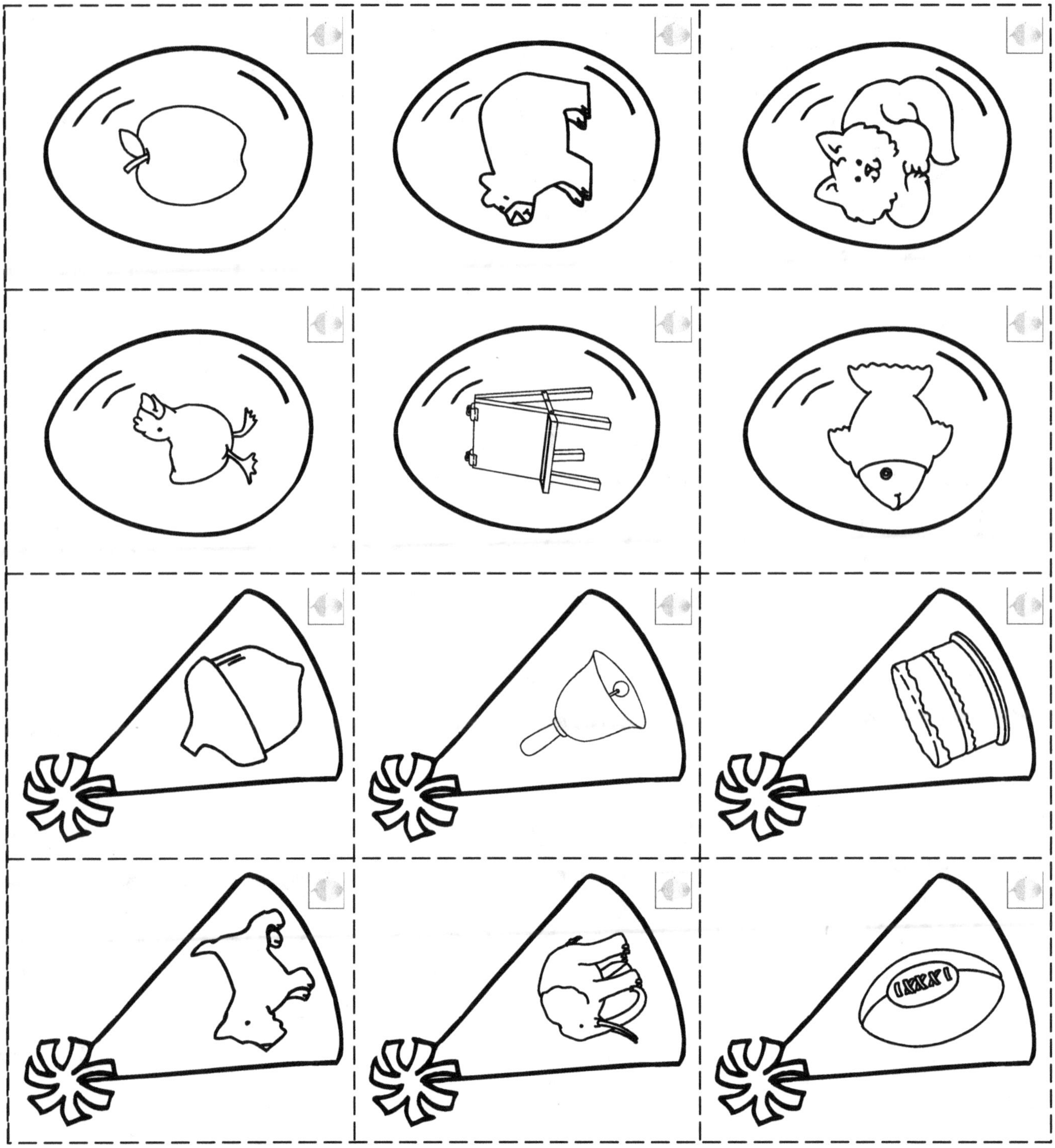

Trail Game

Reproduce, color, and cut apart two sets of cards.

Who's There?

Matching Pictures to Letters F-K

Match Board

Assembly

Reproduce, cut out, and glue a set of oak tag handles (p. 192) to a standard-size file folder. Option: Decorate each handle with copies of the feathers shown on this page. Reproduce, color, and cut out the "Who's There?" patterns. Glue the match boards to the inside of the folder. Glue the cover art to the front of the folder. Decorate the border around the match boards, then laminate. Reproduce, color, laminate, then cut apart four sets of game cards. Glue an envelope to the back of the folder for game card storage. Option: Reproduce, cut out, and glue the Match Board Playing Directions to the back of the folder.

Who's There? Cover

Matching Pictures to Letters F-K

Match Board

Who's There?

Who's There?
Matching Pictures to Letters F-K

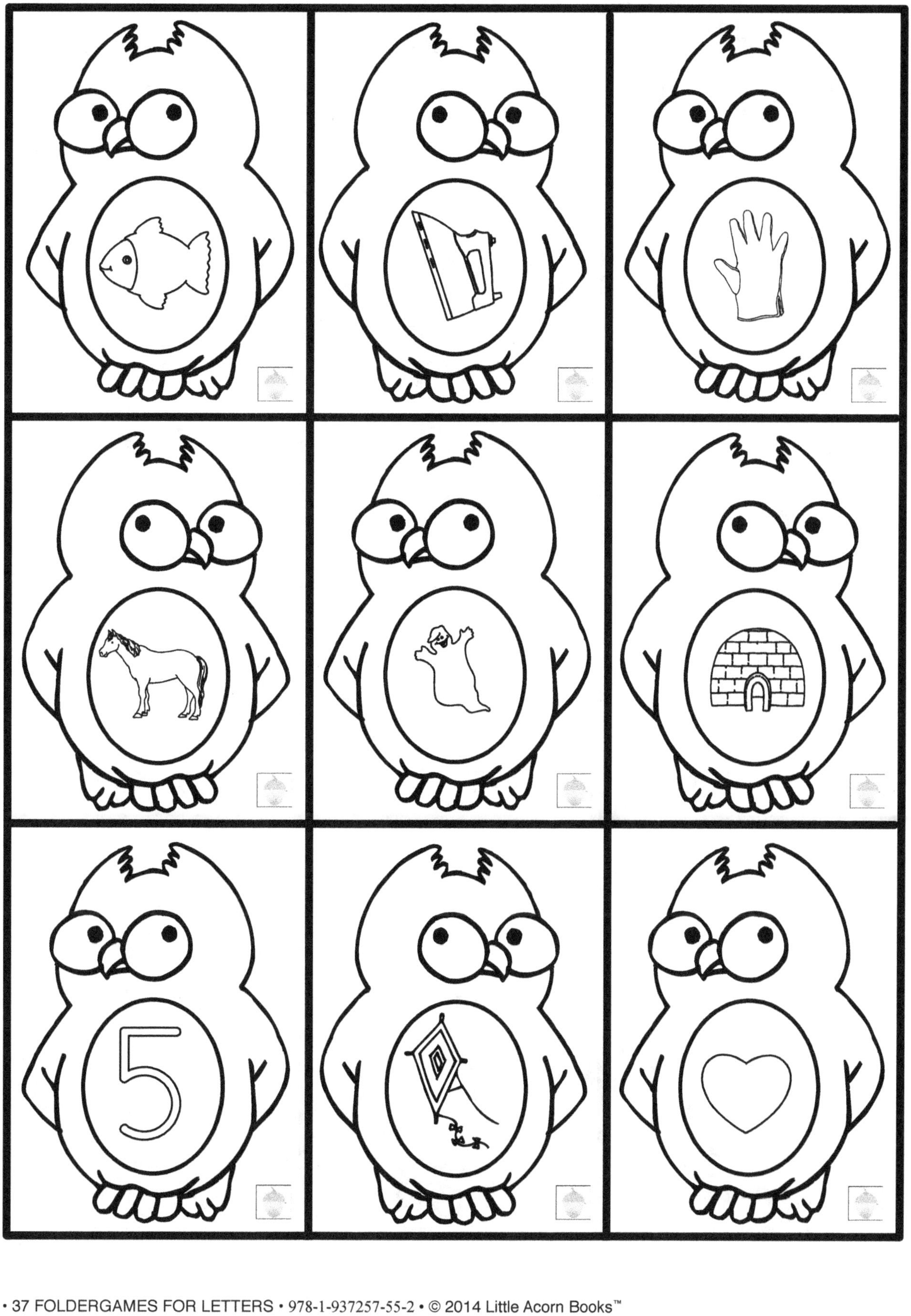

Match Board

23

Who's There?
Matching Pictures to Letters F-K

Match Board

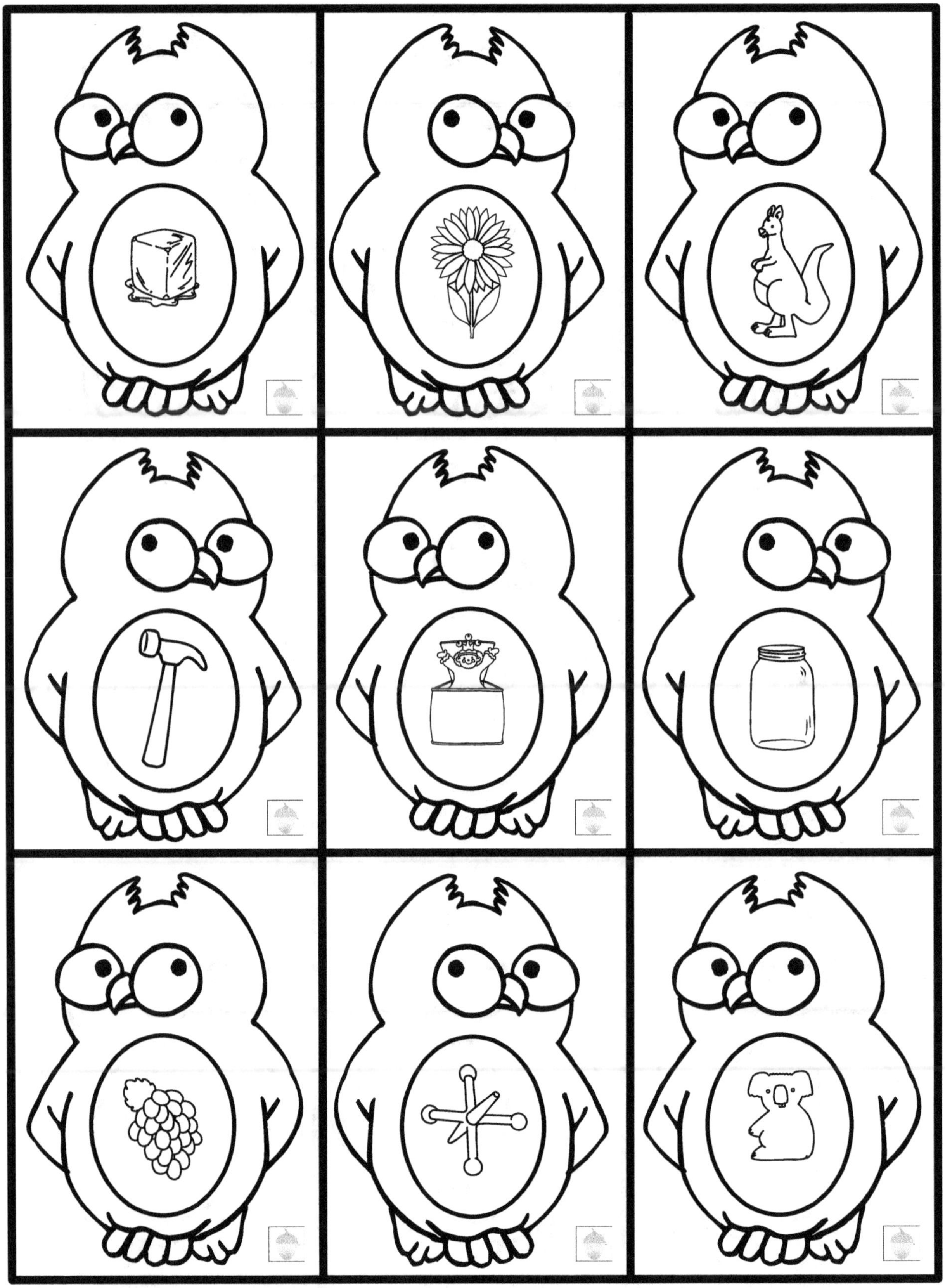

Who's There?
Matching Pictures to Letters F-K

Match Board

F G H
I J K

Reproduce, color, and cut apart four sets of cards.

Alligator Tails
Matching Pictures to Letters K-P

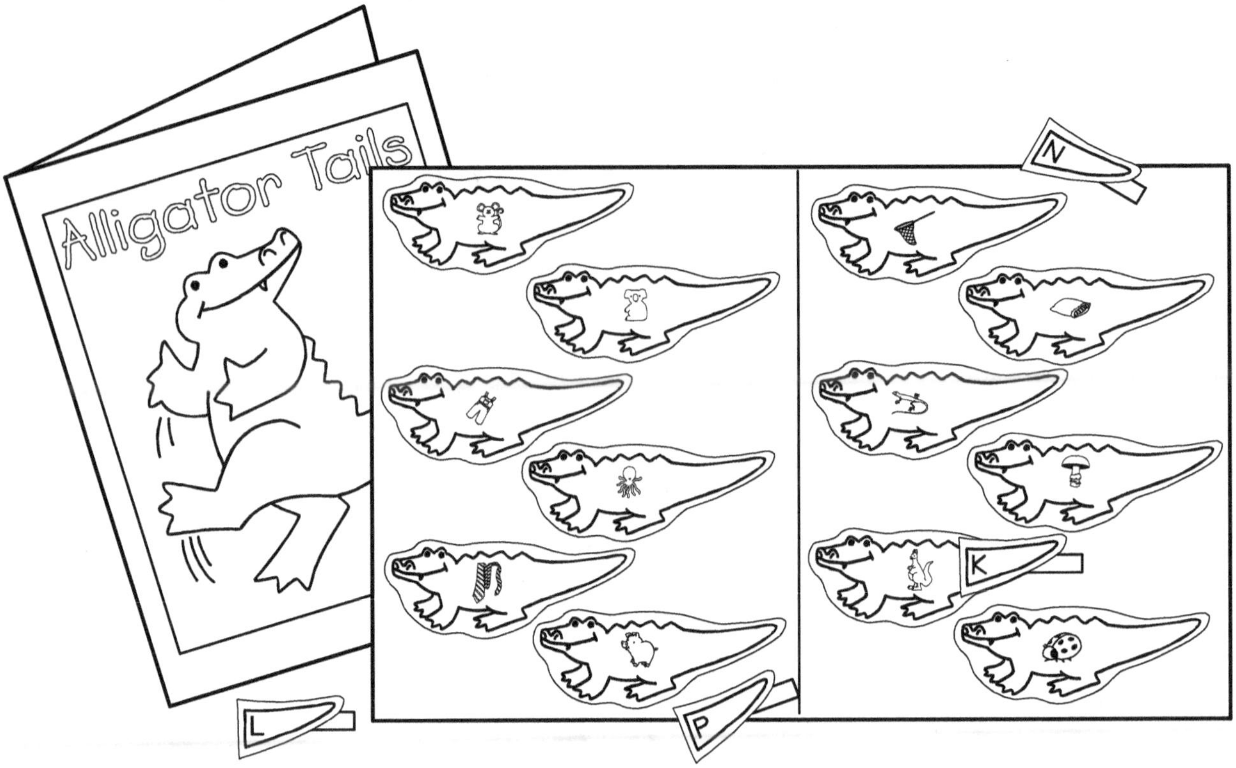

Clothespin Match-ups

Assembly

Reproduce, cut out, and glue a set of green poster board handles (p. 192) to a standard-size file folder. Option: Decorate the handles with copies of the alligators shown on this page. Reproduce, color, and cut out the "Alligator Tails" patterns. Glue the alligator tails on clothespins. Arrange and glue the assembled alligators to the inside of the folder. Glue the cover to the front of the folder. Decorate the border around the alligators. Staple a resealable plastic bag to the back of the folder for clothespin storage. Option: Reproduce, cut out, and glue the Clothespin Match-ups Playing Directions to the back of the folder.

Alligator Tails Cover
Matching Pictures to Letters K-P
Clothespin Match-ups

Alligator Tails

Alligator Tails

Matching Pictures to Letters K-P

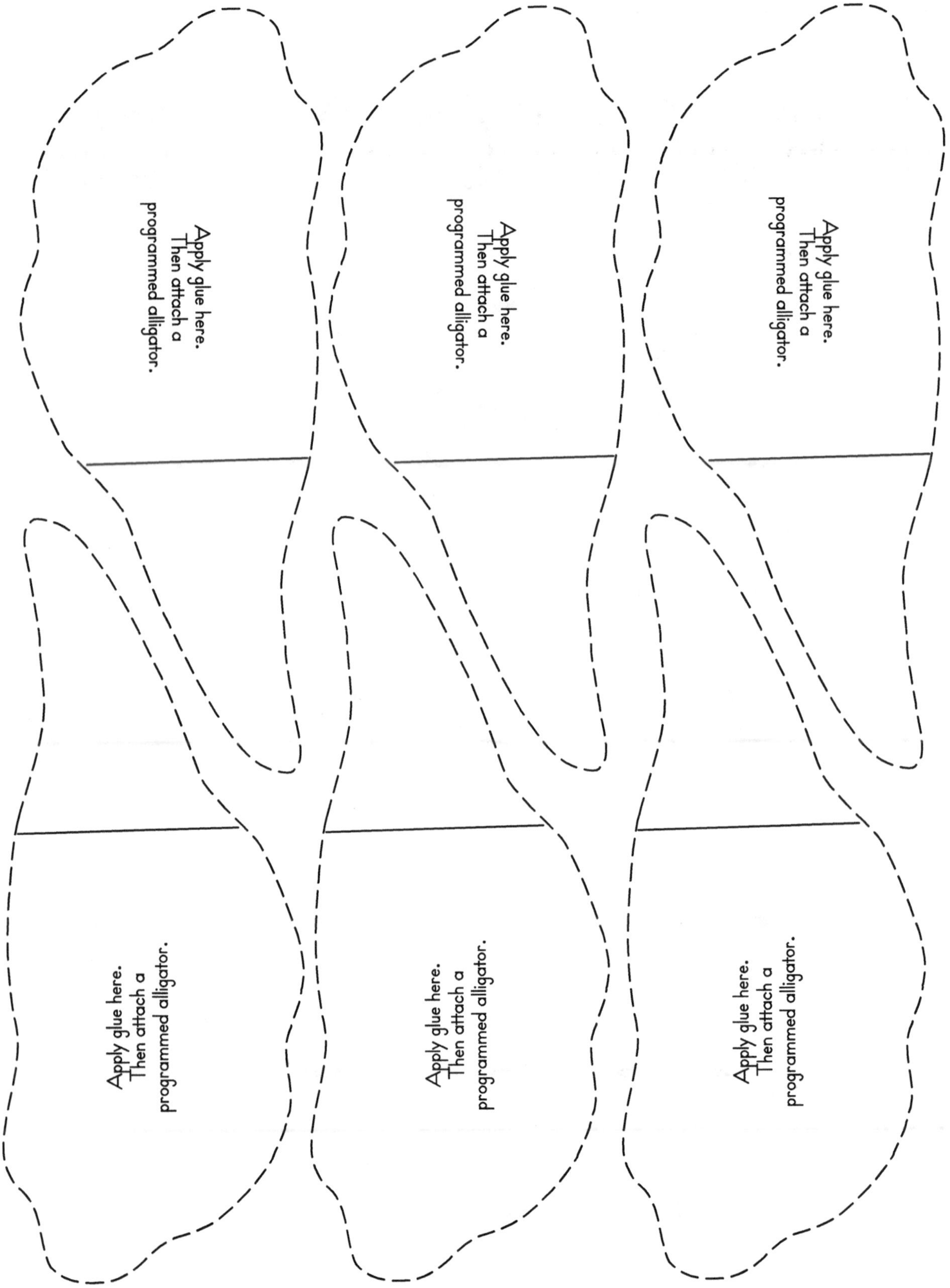
Apply glue here.
Then attach a
programmed alligator.
Apply glue here.
Then attach a
programmed alligator.
Apply glue here.
Then attach a
programmed alligator.
Apply glue here.
Then attach a
programmed alligator.
Apply glue here.
Then attach a
programmed alligator.
Apply glue here.
Then attach a
programmed alligator.

Reproduce, cut out, and glue 12 alligator outlines to the inside of a folder.
Do not glue down alligator tails.

LAB20146P • 37 FOLDERGAMES FOR LETTERS • 978-1-937257-55-2 •

Alligator Tails
Matching Pictures to Letters K-P

Clothespin Match-ups

Reproduce, color, cut out, and glue each alligator to an alligator outline.
Do not glue down alligator tails.

Alligator Tails
Matching Pictures to Letters K-P

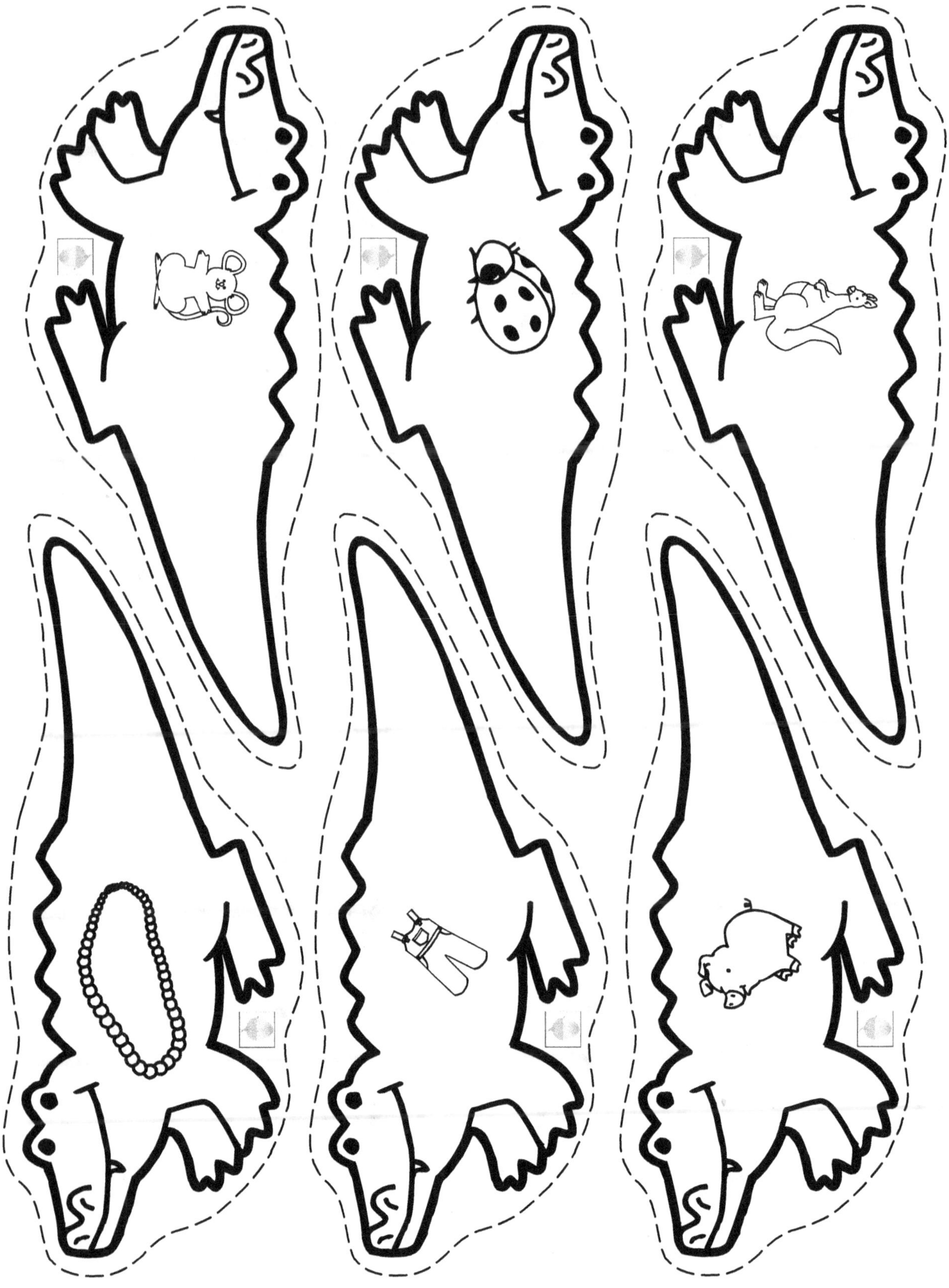

Clothespin Match-ups

Reproduce, color, cut out, and glue each alligator to an alligator outline.
Do not glue down alligator tails.

Alligator Tails
Matching Pictures to Letters K-P

Clothespin Match-ups

Reproduce, color, cut out, and glue each alligator tail on a clothespin.

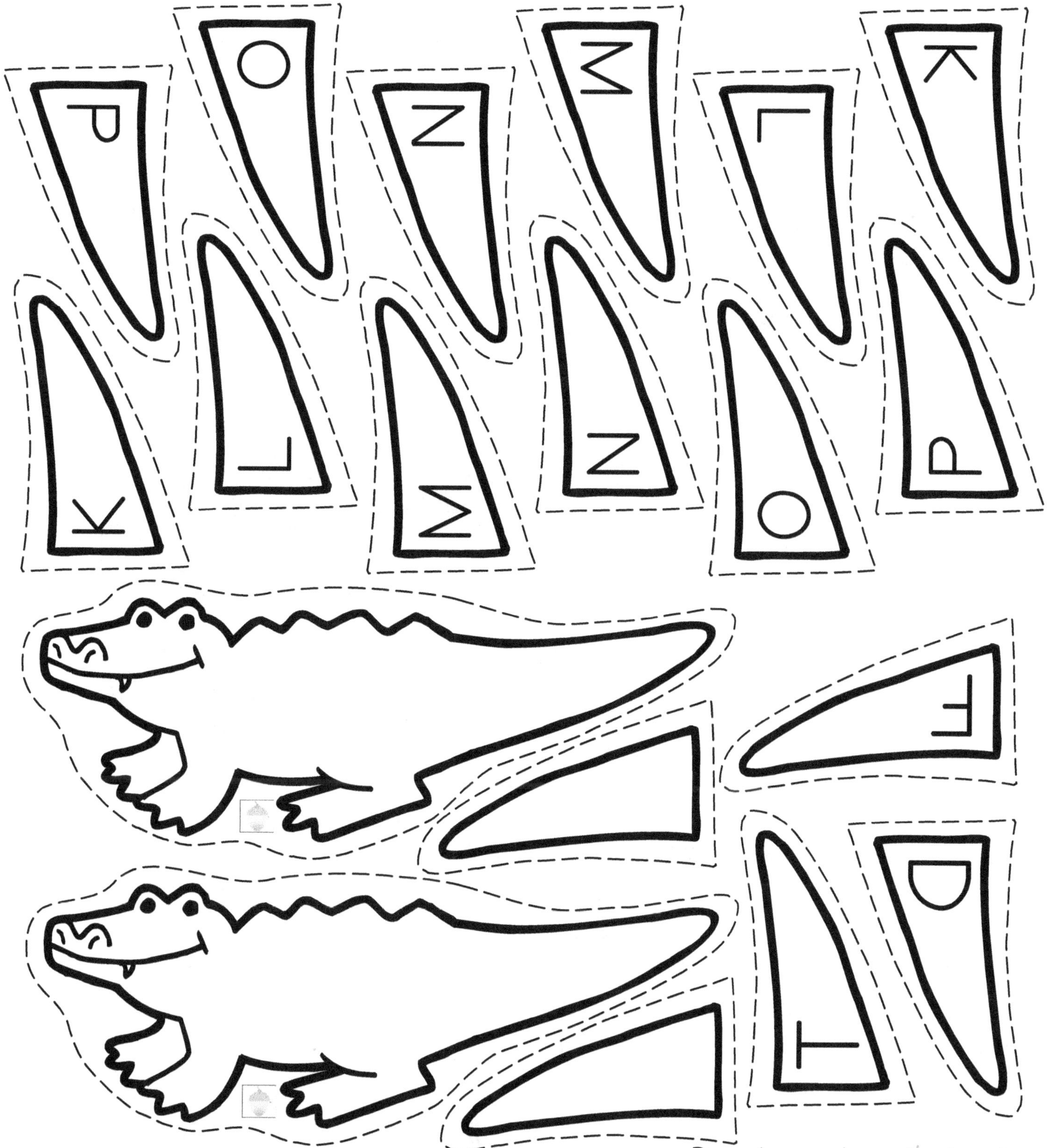

Option: Reproduce and program blank alligators and tails with additional alphabet pictures.

Reproduce, color, cut out, and glue these tails on clothespins for advanced skills practice.

Butterfly Dominoes
Matching Pictures to Letters P-U

Dominoes

Assembly

Reproduce, cut out, and glue a set of oak tag handles (p. 192) to a standard-size file folder. Option: Decorate the handles with copies of the butterflies shown on this page. Reproduce, color, and cut out the "Butterfly Dominoes" patterns. Make extra sets of dominoes to accommodate more players. Glue the cover art to the front of the folder. Decorate the inside of the folder, then laminate. Reproduce, color, laminate, then cut apart the dominoes. Glue an envelope to the back of the folder to store dominoes. Option: Reproduce, cut out, and glue the Dominoes Playing Directions to the back of the folder.

Butterfly Dominoes Cover
Matching Pictures to Letters P-U

Dominoes

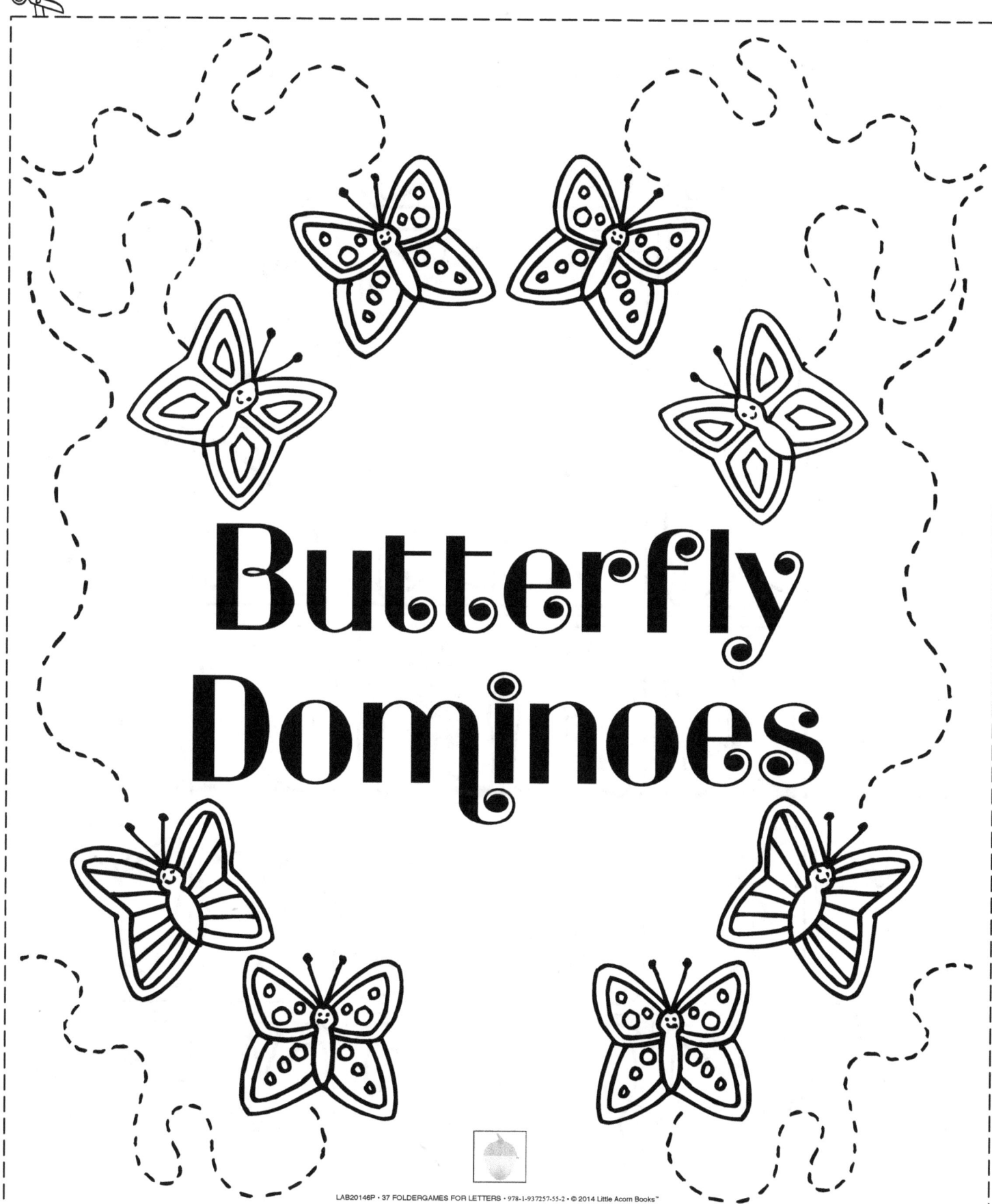

Butterfly Dominoes
Matching Pictures to Letters P-U

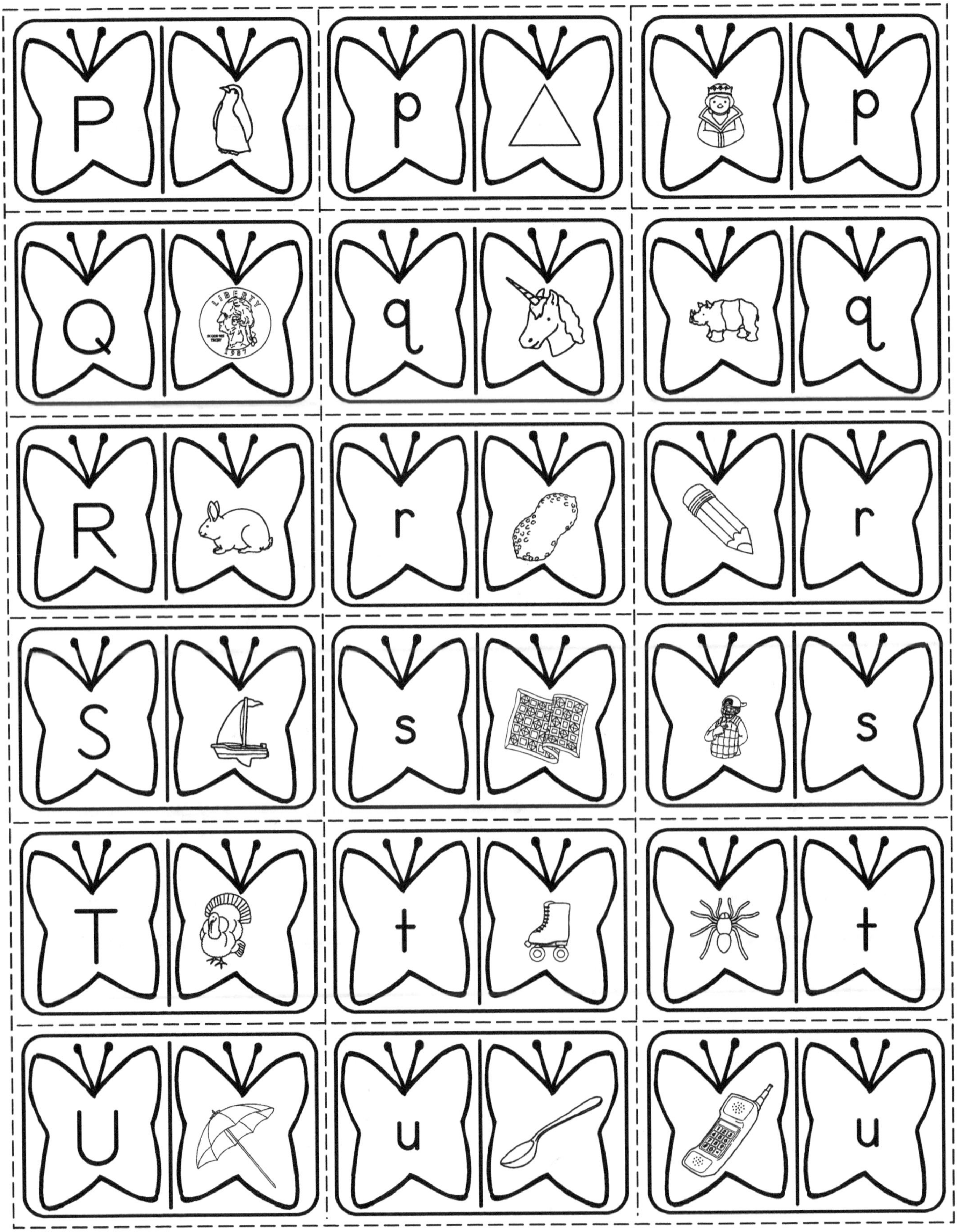

Dominoes

Butterfly Dominoes
Matching Pictures to Letters P-U

Dominoes

Cookie Jar Lotto
Matching Pictures to Letters U-Z

Lotto

Assembly

Reproduce, cut out, and glue a set of oak tag handles (p. 192) to a standard-size file folder. Option: Decorate each handle with copies of the cookies shown on this page. Reproduce, color, and cut out the "Cookie Jar Lotto" patterns. Glue the cover art to the front of the folder. Mount Lotto boards on colored construction paper, then laminate. Glue two envelopes to the inside of the folder for Lotto board, token, and card storage. Option: Reproduce, cut out, and glue the Lotto Playing Directions to the back of the folder. Note: Wipe-off markers or crayons can also be used to color in matches.

Cookie Jar Lotto Cover
Matching Pictures to Letters U–Z

Lotto

Cookie Jar Lotto
Matching Pictures to Letters U-Z

Lotto

Cookie Jar Lotto
Matching Pictures to Letters U-Z

Lotto

Cookie Jar Lotto
Matching Pictures to Letters U-Z

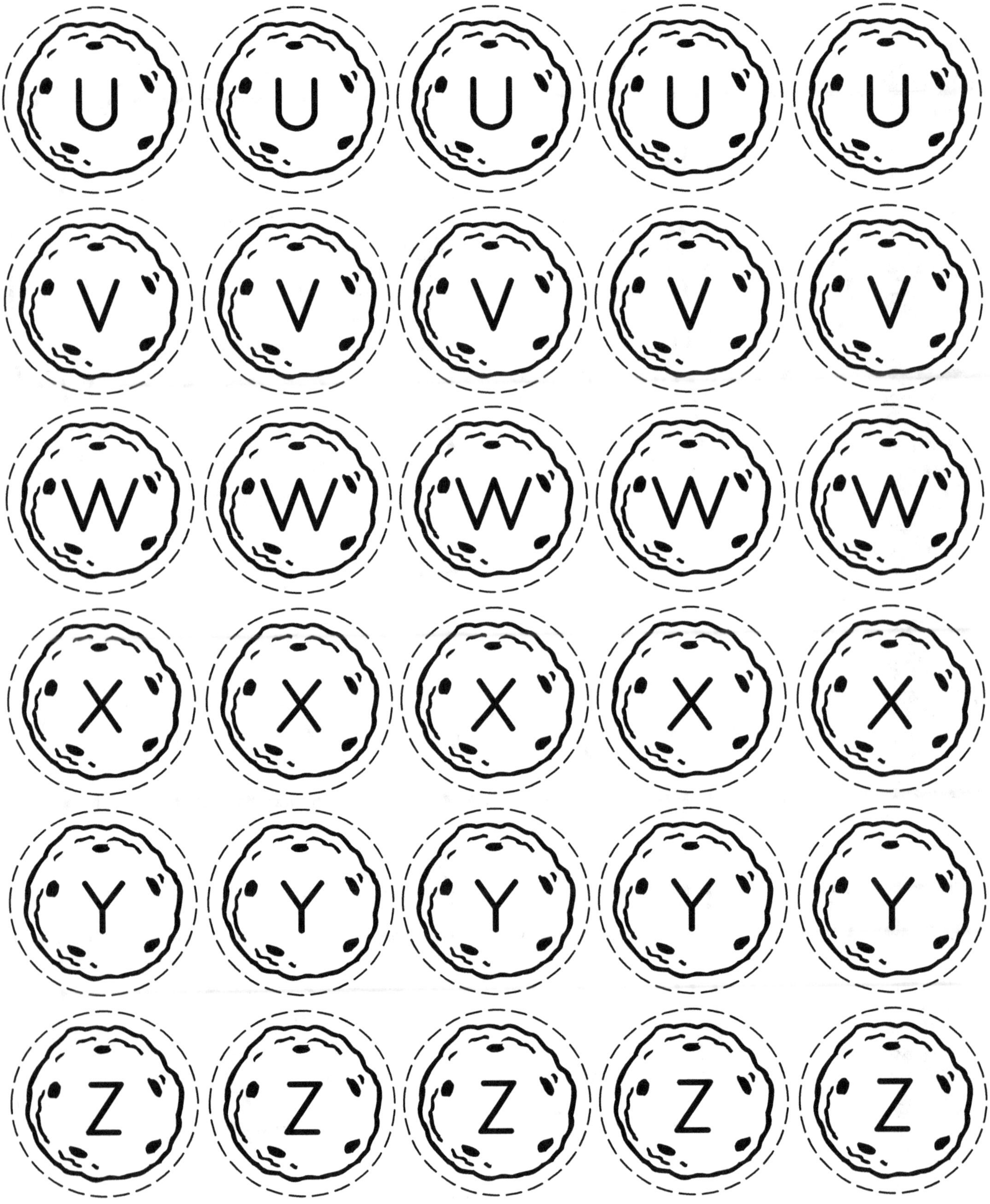

Lotto

U	U	U	U	U
V	V	V	V	V
W	W	W	W	W
X	X	X	X	X
Y	Y	Y	Y	Y
Z	Z	Z	Z	Z

Crayon Wheel

Clothespin Wheel

Matching Uppercase and Lowercase Letters A-F

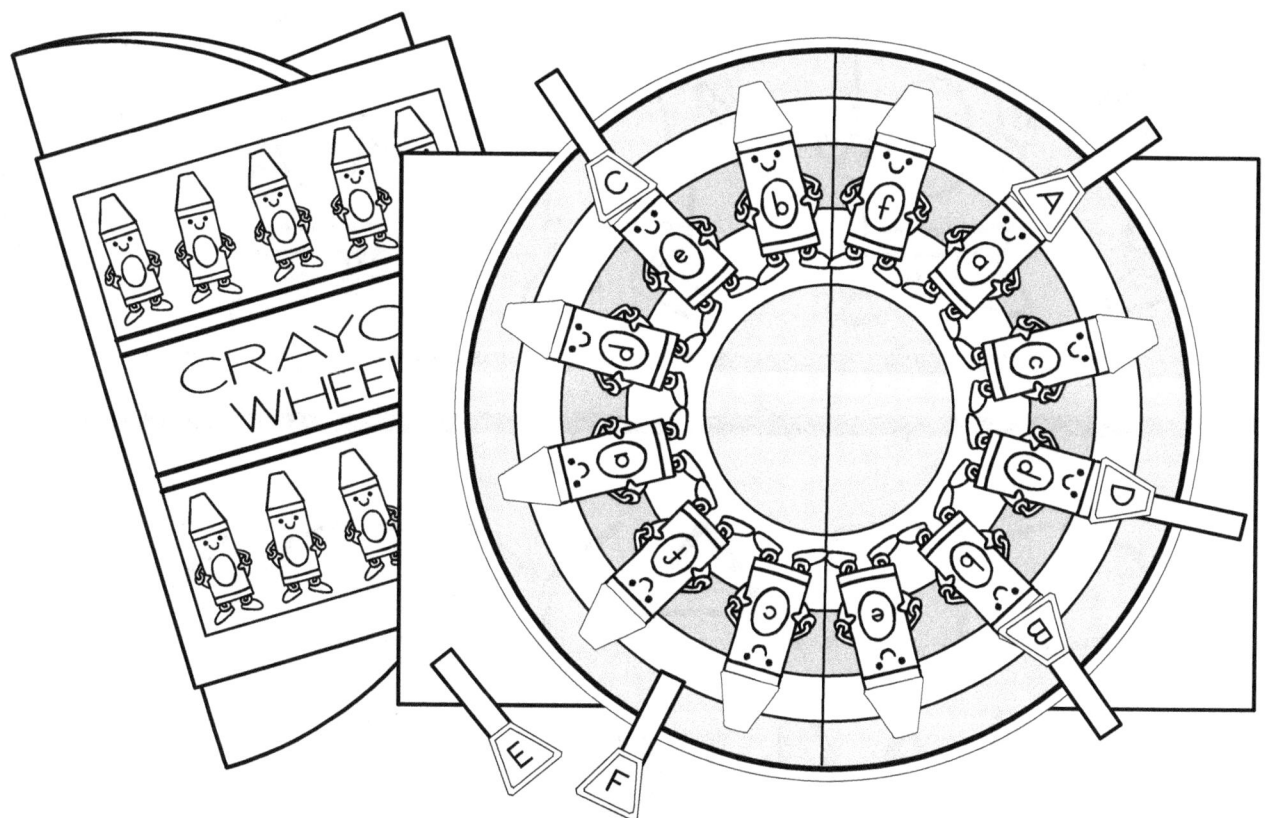

Assembly

Reproduce, cut out, and glue a set of oak tag handles (p. 192) to a standard-size file folder. Option: Decorate the handles with copies of the crayons shown on this page. Reproduce, color, and cut out the "Crayon Wheel" patterns. Glue the cover art to the front of the folder. Staple a resealable plastic bag to the back of the folder for clothespin storage. Glue the crayon tops on clothespins. Meeting along the straight edges, glue the crayon wheel quarters on a large poster board circle. Glue the wheel inside the folder, then glue the programmed crayons on the wheel. Option: Reproduce, cut out, and glue the Clothespin Wheel Playing Directions to the back of the folder.

Crayon Wheel Cover
Matching Uppercase and Lowercase Letters A-F

Clothespin Wheel

CRAYON WHEEL

Crayon Wheel
Matching Uppercase and Lowercase Letters A-F

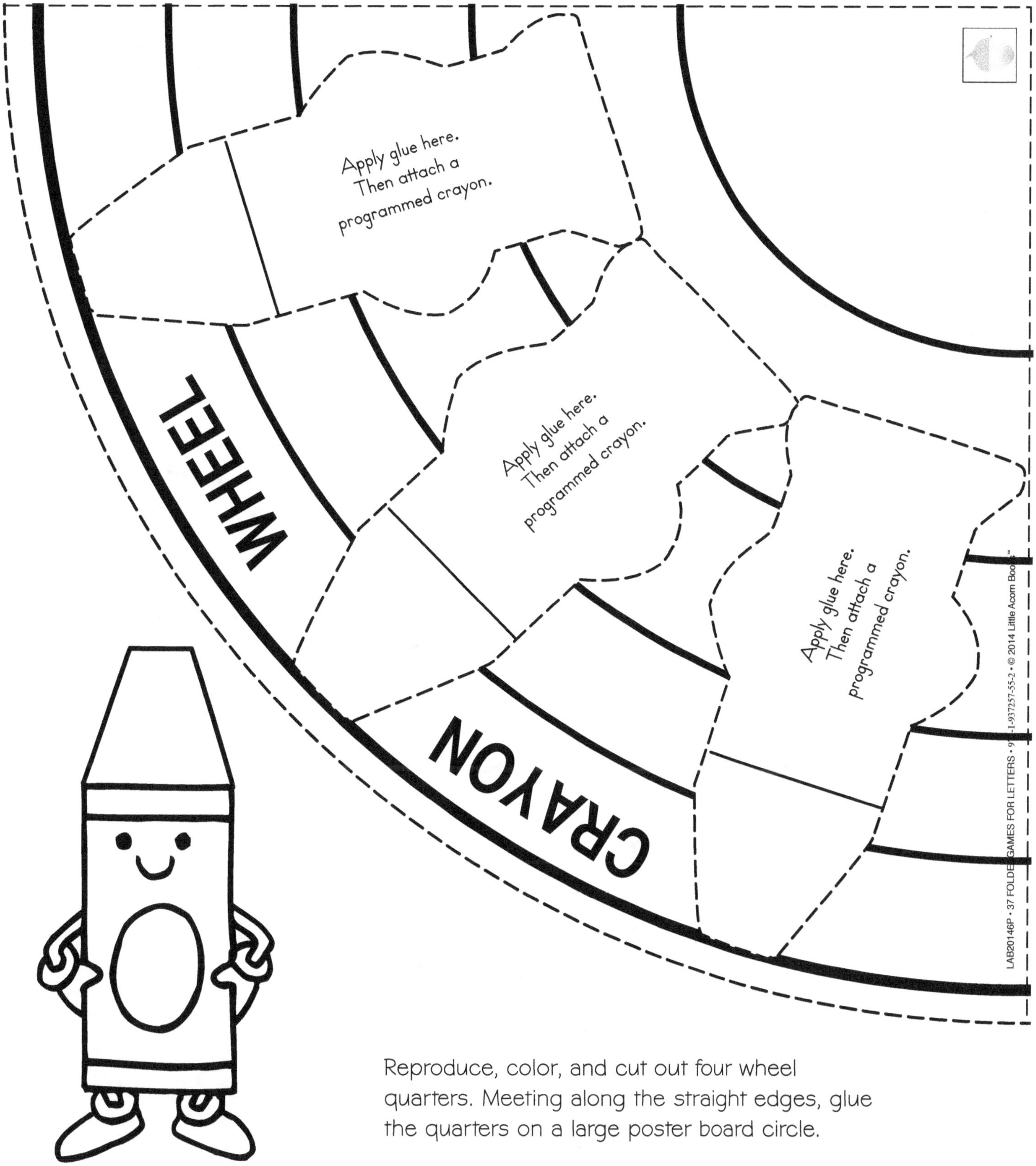

Clothespin Wheel

Apply glue here. Then attach a programmed crayon.

Apply glue here. Then attach a programmed crayon.

Apply glue here. Then attach a programmed crayon.

WHEEL

CRAYON

Reproduce, color, and cut out four wheel quarters. Meeting along the straight edges, glue the quarters on a large poster board circle.

Crayon Wheel
Matching Uppercase and Lowercase Letters • A-F

Clothespin Wheel

Reproduce, color, cut out, and glue two sets of crayon tops on clothespins.

Reproduce, color, cut out, and glue two sets of crayons on the clothespin wheel. Do not glue down the crayon tops

Reproduce, color, cut out, and glue these tops on clothespins for advanced skills practice.

Star Hoppers

Matching Uppercase and Lowercase Letters F–K

Match Board

Assembly

Reproduce, cut out, and glue a set of oak tag handles (p. 192) to a standard-size file folder. Option: Decorate each handle with star stickers or copies of the stars shown on this page. Reproduce, color, and cut out the "Star Hoppers" patterns. Matching in the center, glue the match board patterns to the inside of the folder. Glue the cover art to the front of the folder. Decorate the border around the game board, then laminate. Reproduce, color, laminate, then cut out two sets of game cards. Glue an envelope to the back of the folder for game card storage. Option: Reproduce, cut out, and glue the Match Board Playing Directions to the back of the folder.

Star Hoppers Cover
Matching Uppercase and Lowercase Letters F-K

Match Board

Star Hoppers
Matching Uppercase and Lowercase Letters F–K

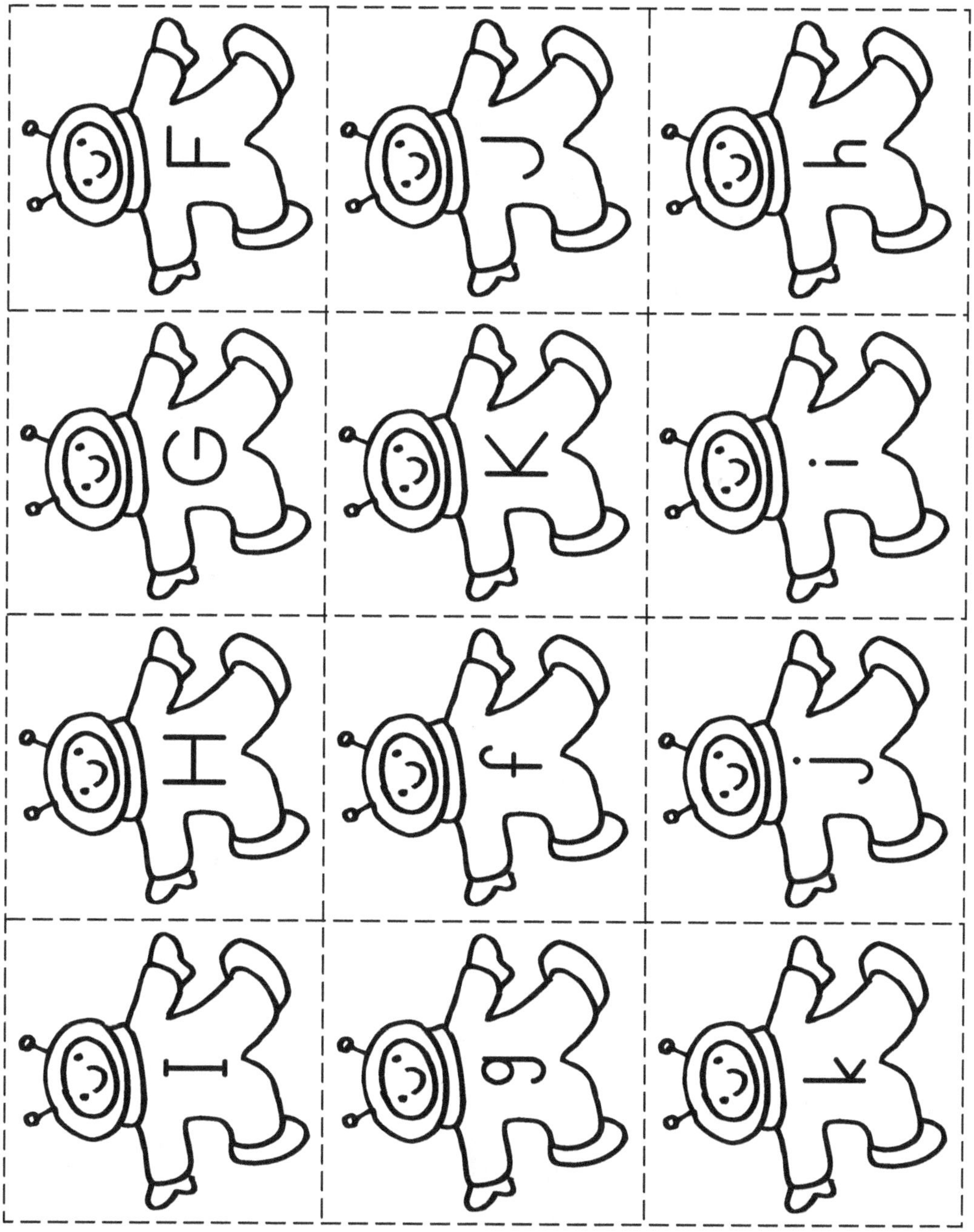

Match Board

Reproduce, color, and cut apart these star hoppers for advanced skills practice.

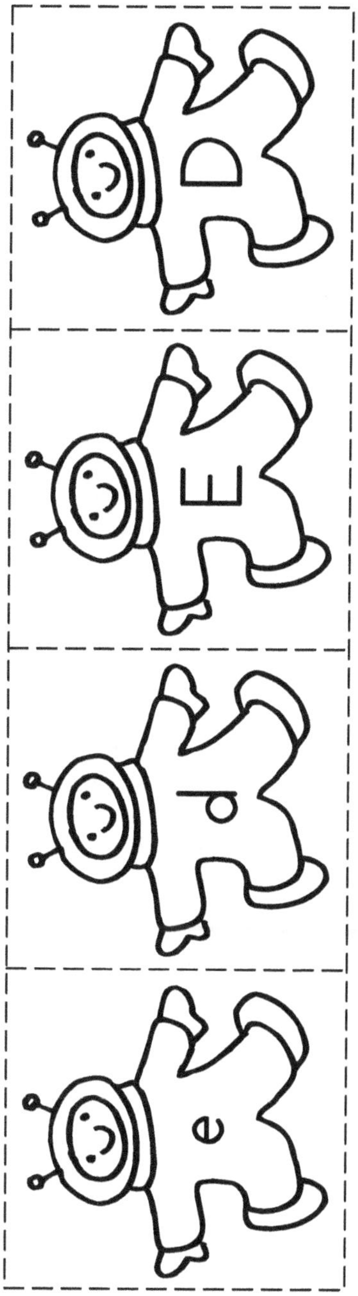

Reproduce, color, and cut apart two sets of cards.

Star Hoppers
Matching Uppercase and Lowercase Letters F-K

Match Board

Star Hoppers

k	F	i
f	j	G
J	h	F
H	I	g

Star Hoppers
Matching Uppercase and Lowercase Letters F-K

Match Board

g	h	K
i	k	j
H	G	K
J	f	I

Leaping Lizards

Trail Game

Matching Uppercase and Lowercase Letters K-P

Assembly

Reproduce, cut out, and glue a set of oak tag handles (p. 192) to a standard-size file folder. Option: Decorate each handle with bright color polka-dots. Reproduce, color, and cut out the "Leaping Lizards" patterns. Matching in the center, glue the game board patterns to the inside of the folder. Glue the cover art to the front of the folder. Decorate the border around the game board, then laminate. Reproduce, color, laminate, then cut out the pawns and two sets of game cards. Glue an envelope to the back of the folder for pawn and game card storage. Option: Reproduce, cut out, and glue the Trail Game Playing Directions to the back of the folder.

Pawns

Leaping Lizards Cover
Matching Uppercase and Lowercase Letters K-P

Trail Game

Leaping Lizards
Matching Uppercase and Lowercase Letters • K-P

Trail Game

Leaping Lizards
Matching Uppercase and Lowercase Letters K-P

Trail Game

Help the lizards leap to the end of the mushroom trail.

Leaping Lizards
Matching Uppercase and Lowercase Letters K-P

Trail Game

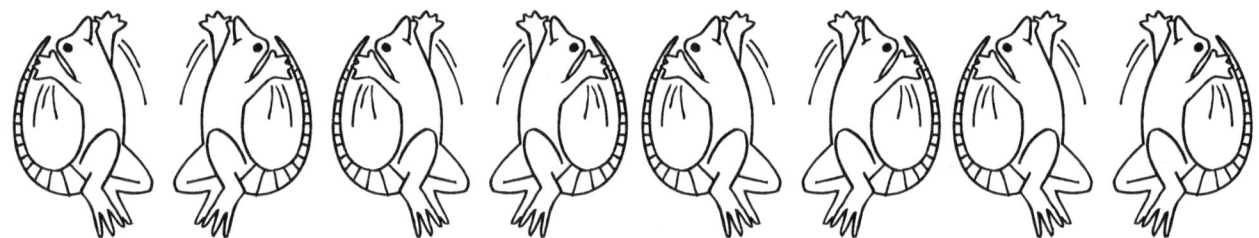

Reproduce, color, and cut apart two sets of mushroom cards.

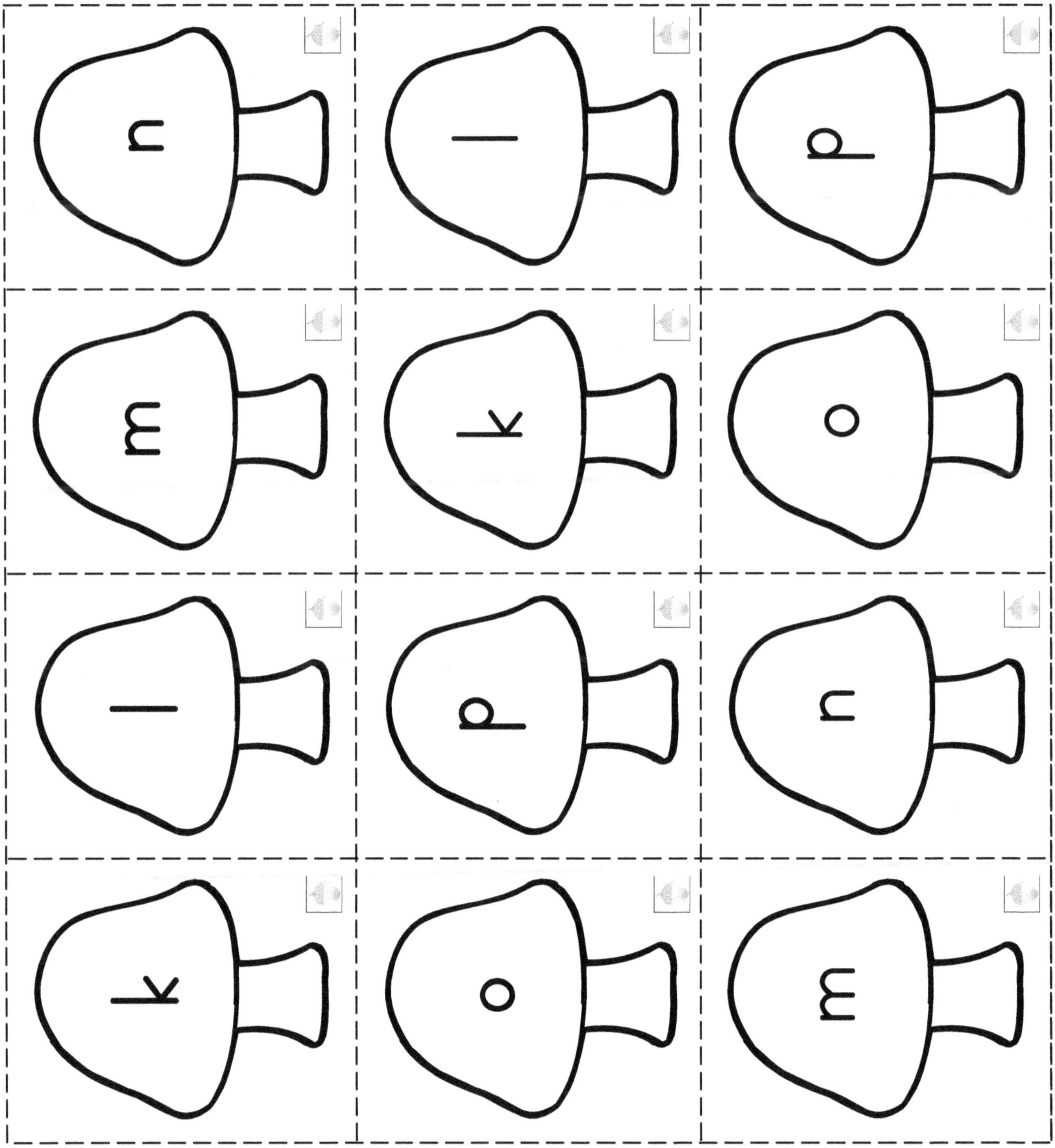

n	l	p
m	k	o
l	p	n
k	o	m

Peek-a-boo Bunnies

Pocket Game

Matching Uppercase and Lowercase Letters P-U

Assembly

Reproduce, cut out, and glue a set of oak tag handles (p. 192) to a standard-size file folder. Option: Decorate each handle with a copy of the bunnies on this page. Reproduce, color, and cut out the "Peek-a-boo Bunnies" patterns. Glue two placement templates to the inside of the folder. Apply glue only along the bottom and side edges, then attach five baskets to each template. Glue the cover art to the front of the folder. Decorate the border around the game board. Glue an envelope to the back of the folder for bunny storage. Option: Reproduce, cut out, and glue the Pocket Game Playing Directions to the back of the folder. Note: Make additional "Peek-a-boo Bunnies" pocket folders with different combinations of baskets.

Peek-a-boo Bunnies Cover
Matching Uppercase and Lowercase Letters P-U

Pocket Game

Peek-a-boo Bunnies

Peek-a-boo Bunnies
Matching Uppercase and Lowercase Letters P-U

Pocket Game

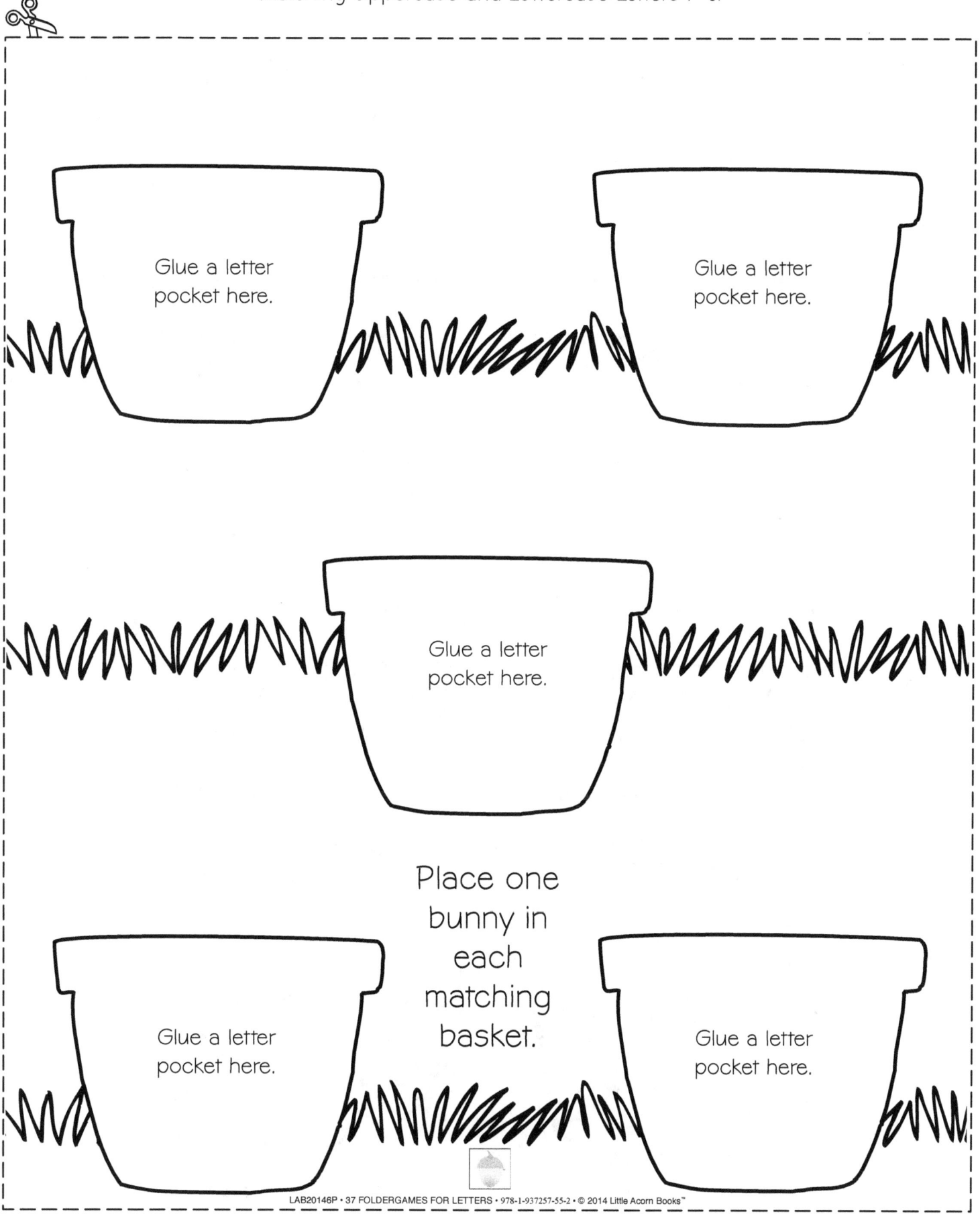

Peek-a-boo Bunnies

Pocket Game

Matching Uppercase and Lowercase Letters P-U

Reproduce, color, and cut out, two sets of baskets.
Apply glue only along the bottom and side edges of each letter basket.
Then attach each basket to a placement template.

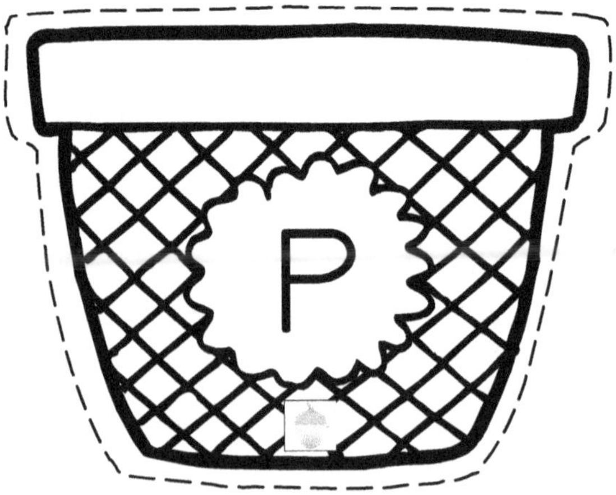

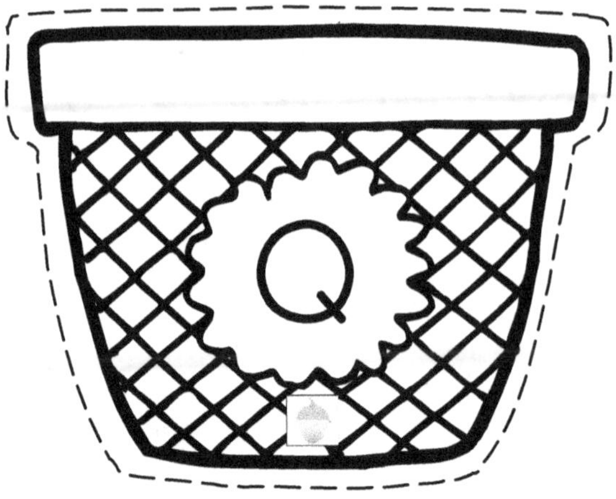

S   P

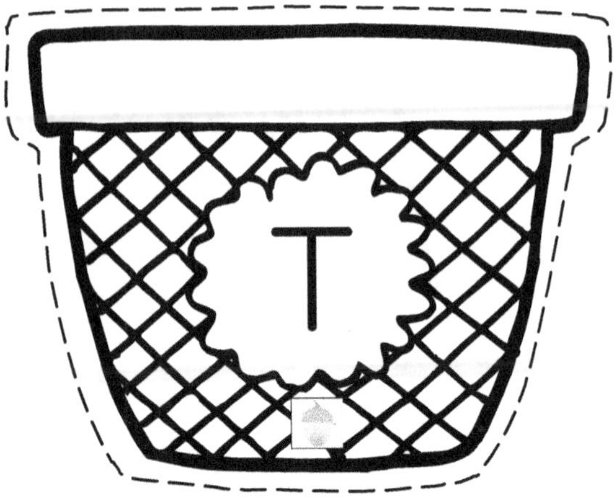

T   Q

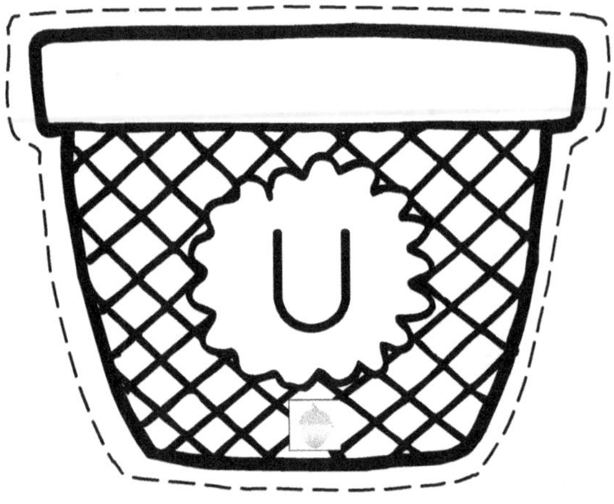

U   R

58   LAB20146P • 37 FOLDERGAMES FOR LETTERS • 978-1-937257-55-2 • © 2014 Little Acorn Books™

Peek-a-boo Bunnies

Pocket Game

Matching Uppercase and Lowercase Letters P-U

Reproduce, color, and cut out, two sets of letter rabbits.

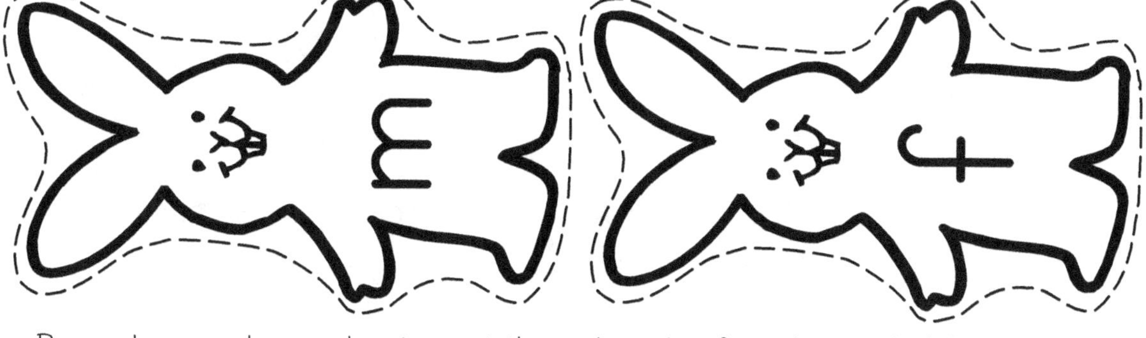

Reproduce, color, and cut apart these bunnies for advanced skills practice.

Popcorn Dominoes

Matching Uppercase and Lowercase Letters U-Z

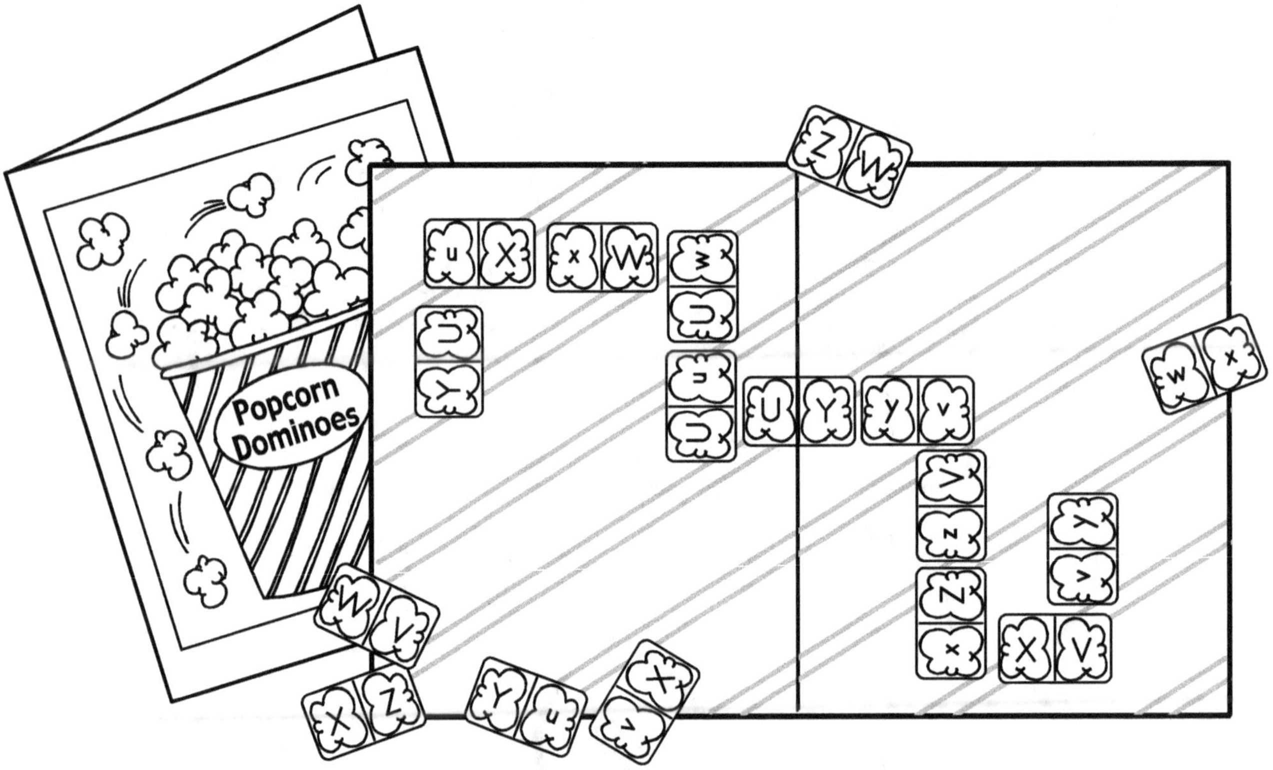

Assembly

Reproduce, cut out, and glue a set of oak tag handles (p. 192) to a standard-size file folder. Option: Draw red stripes on the handles or decorate with copies of the popcorn shown on this page. Reproduce, color, and cut out the "Popcorn Dominoes" patterns. Make extra sets of dominoes to accommodate more players. Glue the cover art to the front of the folder. Decorate the inside of the folder, then laminate. Reproduce, color, laminate, then cut apart the dominoes. Glue an envelope to the back of the folder to store dominoes. Option: Reproduce, cut out, and glue the Dominoes Playing Directions to the back of the folder.

LAB20146P • 37 FOLDERGAMES FOR LETTERS • 978-1-937257-55-2 •

Popcorn Dominoes Cover
Matching Uppercase and Lowercase Letters U-Z

Dominoes

Popcorn Dominoes
Matching Uppercase and Lowercase Letters U-Z

Dominoes

U	Y	u	z	U	u
V	X	v	y	V	v
W	V	w	x	W	w
X	Z	x	u	X	x
Y	U	y	v	Y	y
Z	W	z	w	Z	z

Popcorn Dominoes
Matching Uppercase and Lowercase Letters U-Z

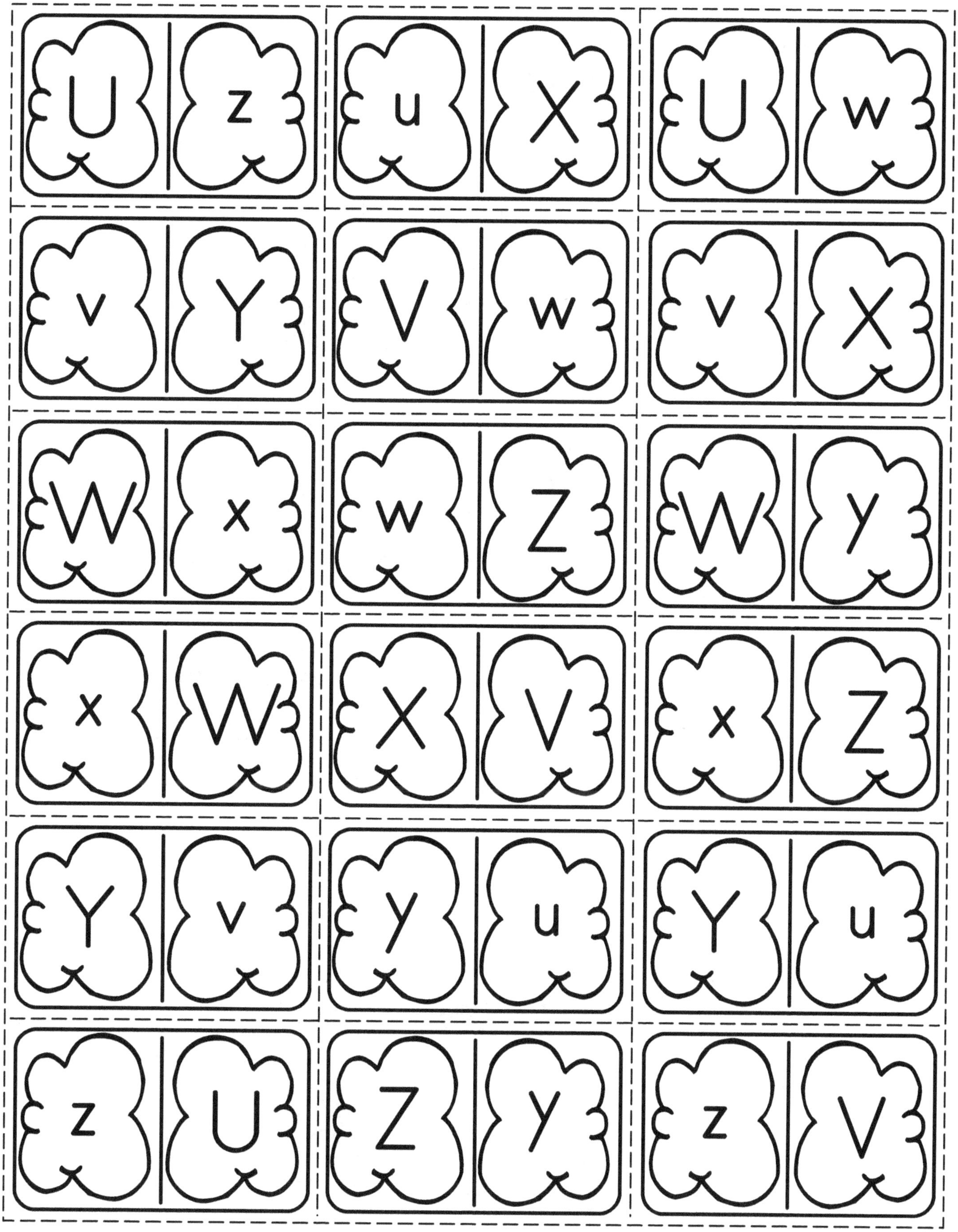

Dominoes

U | z	u | X	U | w
V | Y	V | w	v | X
W | x	w | Z	W | y
x | W	X | V	x | Z
Y | v	y | u	Y | u
z | U	Z | y	z | V

Peas in Pods Cover

Sequencing Letters A-F

Fill-ins

Write the correct missing letters on the pods.

Assembly

Reproduce, cut out, and glue a set of oak tag handles (p. 192) to a standard-size file folder. Option: Draw green polka dots on each handle. Reproduce, color, and cut out the "Peas in Pods" patterns. Glue the fill-in boards to the inside of the folder. Glue the cover art to the front of the folder. Decorate the border around the fill-in boards, then laminate. Glue an envelope to the back of the folder for wipe-off marker or crayon storage. Option: Reproduce, cut out, and glue the Fill-ins Playing Directions to the back of the folder.

Peas in Pods Cover
Sequencing Letters A-F

Fill-ins

Peas in Pods
Sequencing Letters A–F

Fill-ins

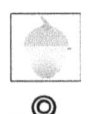

Write the correct missing letters on the pods.

Peas in Pods
Sequencing Letters A-F

Fill-ins

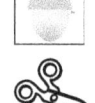

Peas in Pods

Pod 1: C, _, E, _
Pod 2: B, _, D, E, _
Pod 3: _, _, D, _, F
Pod 4: _, D, E, _

Write the correct missing letters on the pods.

LAB20146P • 37 FOLDERGAMES FOR LETTERS • 978-1-937257-55-2 • © 2014 Little Acorn Books™

Peas in Pods
Sequencing Letters A-F

Fill-ins

Reproduce and program additional pea pods for children to fill in missing letters.

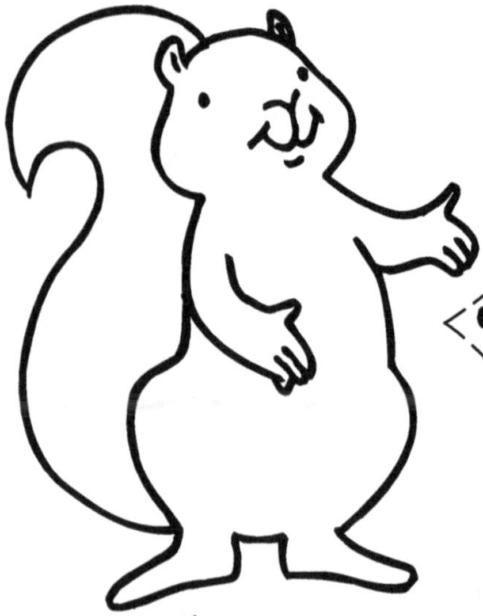

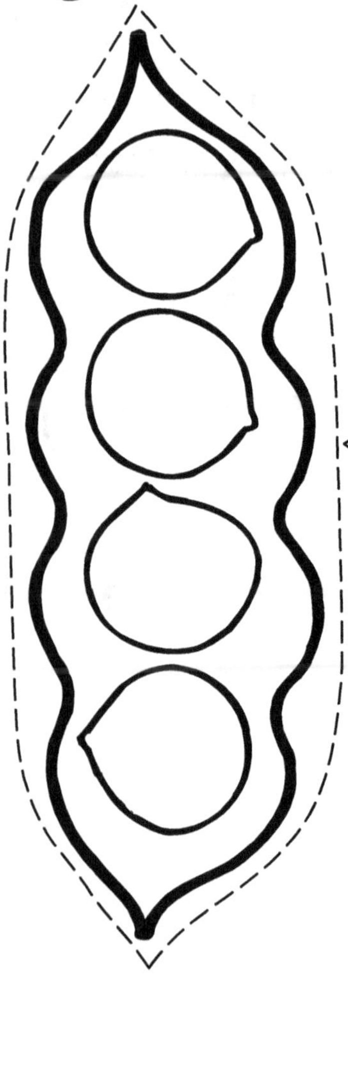

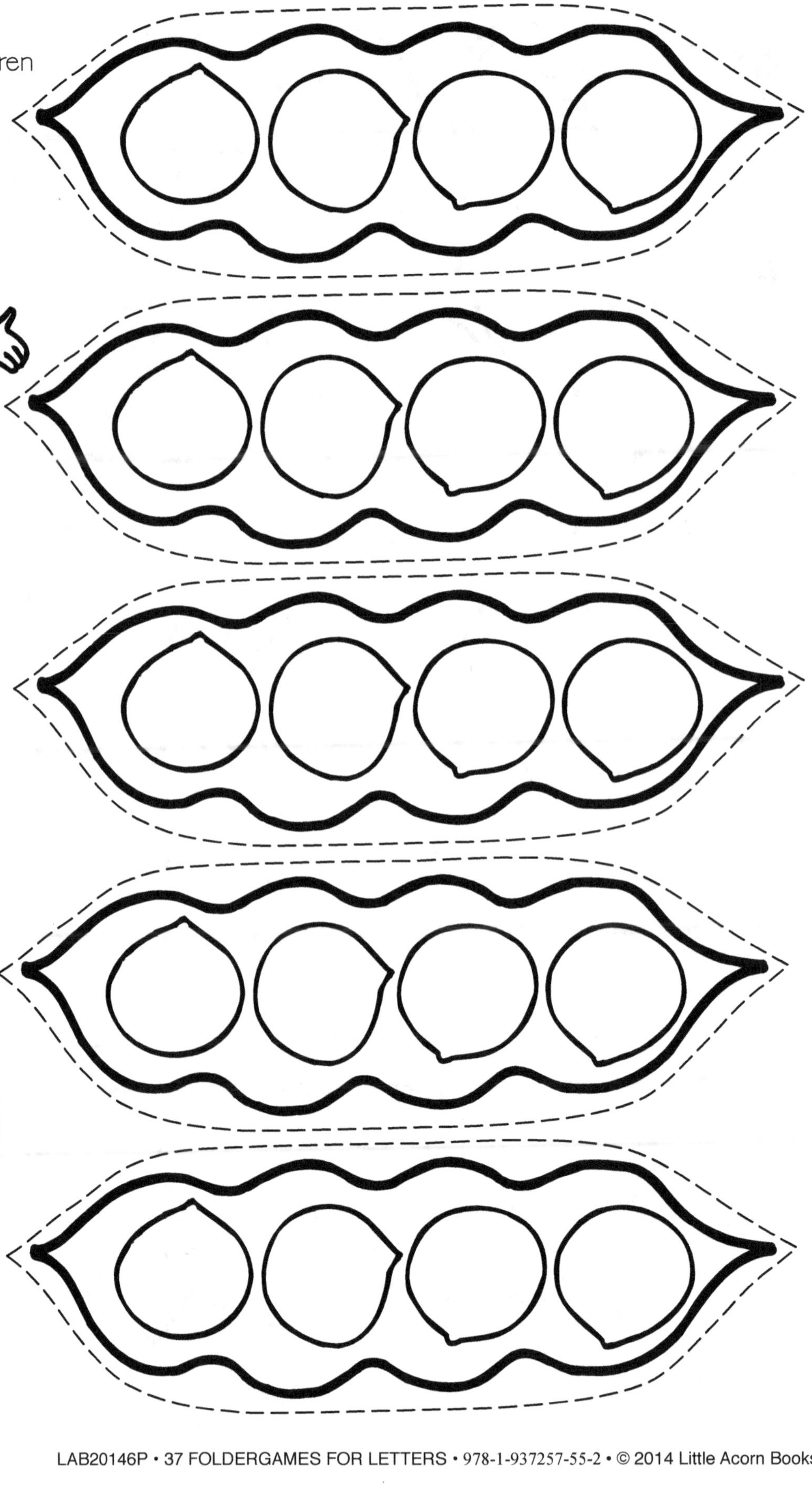

Topsy Turvy Top Hats

Match Board

Sequencing Letters F-O

Assembly

Reproduce, cut out, and glue a set of oak tag handles (p. 192) to a standard-size file folder. Option: Decorate each handle with copies of the hats shown on this page. Reproduce, color, and cut out the "Topsy Turvy Hats" patterns. Glue the match boards to the inside of the folder. Glue the cover art to the front of the folder. Decorate the border around the match boards, then laminate. Reproduce, color, laminate, and cut out the hats. Glue an envelope to the back of the folder for hat storage. Option: Reproduce, cut out, and glue the Match Board Playing Directions to the back of the folder.

Topsy Turvy Top Hats Cover
Sequencing Letters F-O

Match Board

Topsy Turvy Top Hats

Topsy Turvy Top Hats
Sequencing Letters F-O

Match Board

Reproduce, color, and cut out, two sets of letter hats.

f g h i

j k l m

n o

Reproduce and program blank monkey and hat sets for additional alphabet sequencing.

Topsy Turvy Top Hats
Sequencing Letters F-O

Match Board

Topsy Turvy Top Hats
Sequencing Letters F-O

Match Board

Place the correct letter hat next to each monkey.

Topsy Turvy Hats

Sailing, Sailing
Sequencing Letters P-U

Fill-ins

Assembly

Measure, cut, and fold a sheet of poster board to form a tri-fold fill-in game board. Reproduce, color, and cut out the "Sailing, Sailing" patterns. Glue the fill-in boards to the inside of the tri-folder. Glue the cover art to the front of the folder. Decorate the border around the fill-in boards, then laminate. Glue an envelope to the back of the folder for wipe-off marker or crayon storage. Option: Reproduce, cut out, and glue the Fill-ins Playing Directions to the back of the folder.

Sailing, Sailing Cover
Sequencing Letters P-U
Fill-ins

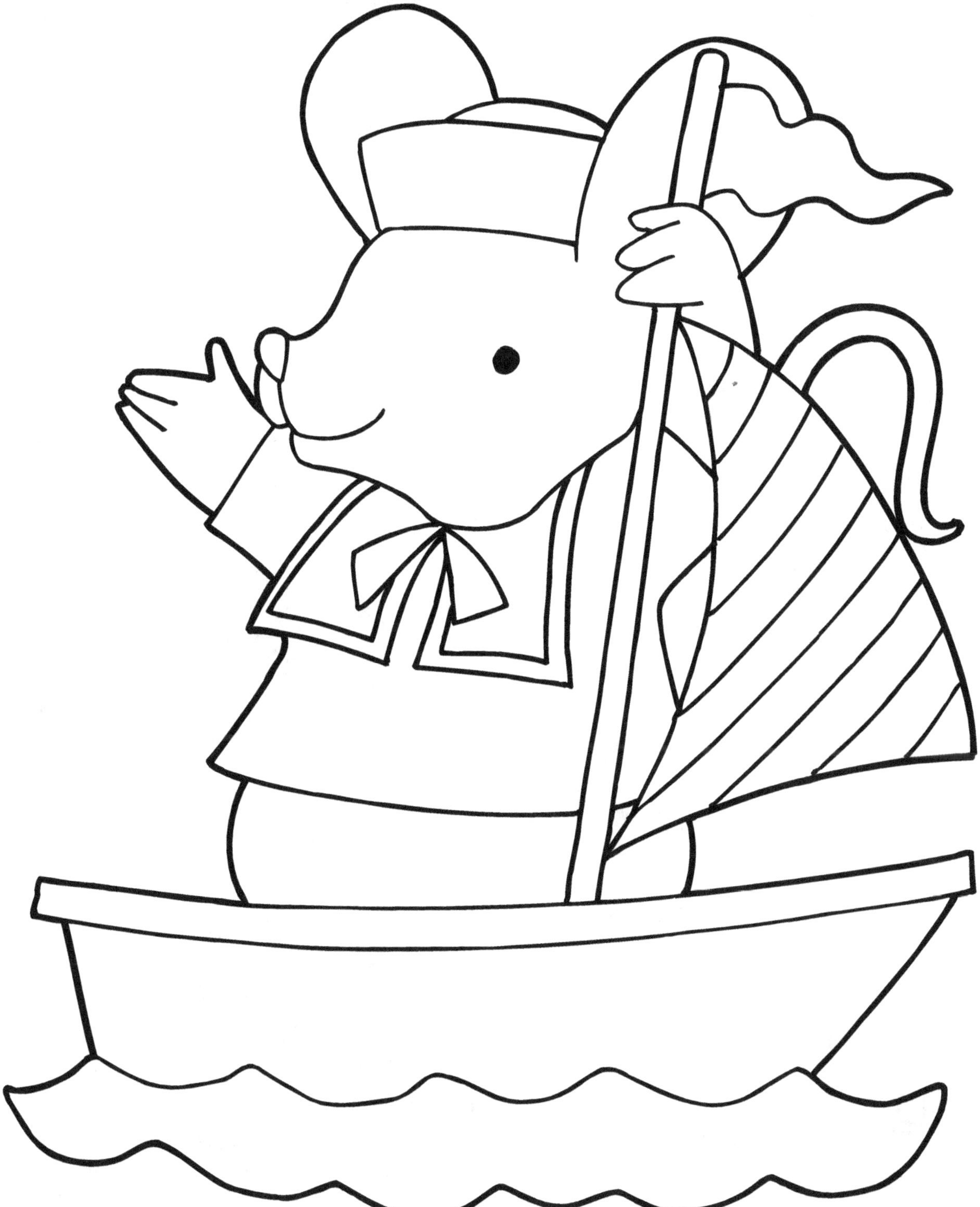

Sailing, Sailing

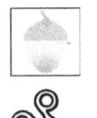

Sailing, Sailing
Sequencing Letters P-U

Fill-ins

Fill in the missing letters.

Boats with letters: P, _, _, S, _, _ (and P, _, R, _, _, _)

Sailing, Sailing
Sequencing Letters P-U

Fill-ins

Fill in the missing letters.

Sailing, Sailing
Sequencing Letters P–U

Fill-ins

Fill in the missing letters.

S
___
___
R
___
Q
___
P

Sailing, Sailing
Sequencing Letters P-U

Fill-ins

Option: Program sailboats with uppercase letter sets: A-F, F-K, K-P, U-Z, then reprogram game boards with matching lowercase letters for an alphabet matching skills practice activity.

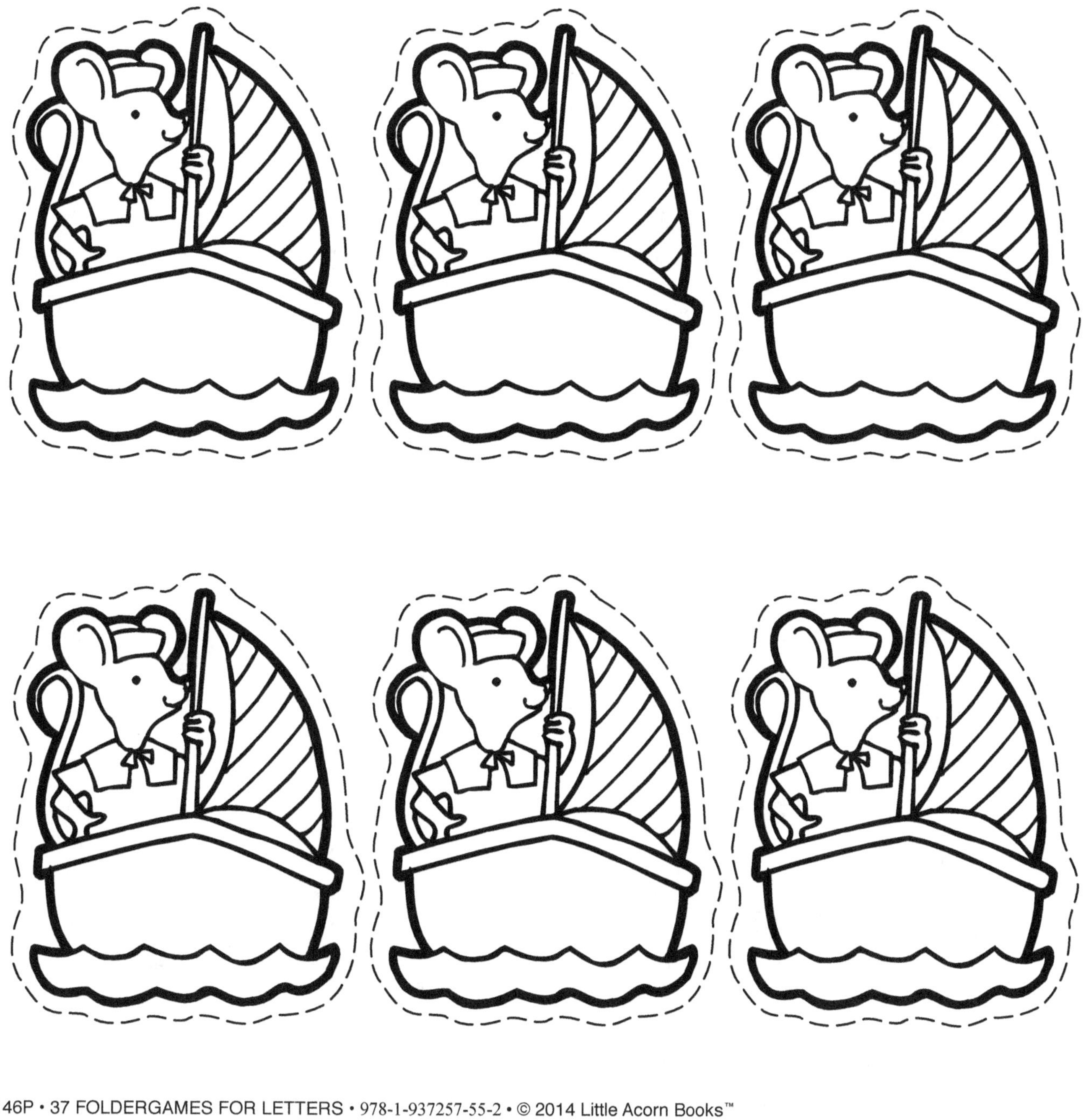

Excellent Elephant

Dot-to-Dot

Sequencing Letters A-Z

Assembly

Reproduce, cut out, and glue a set of oak tag handles (p. 192) to a standard-size file folder. Option: Decorate each handle with a copy of the elephants on this page. Reproduce, color, and cut out the "Excellent Elephant" patterns. Matching in the center, glue the dot-to-dot boards to the inside of the folder. Glue the cover art to the front of the folder, then laminate. Glue an envelope to the back of the folder to store a wipe-off marker or crayon and soft cloth. Option: Reproduce, cut out, and glue the Dot-to-Dot Playing Directions to the back of the folder.

Excellent Elephant Cover
Sequencing Letters A-Z

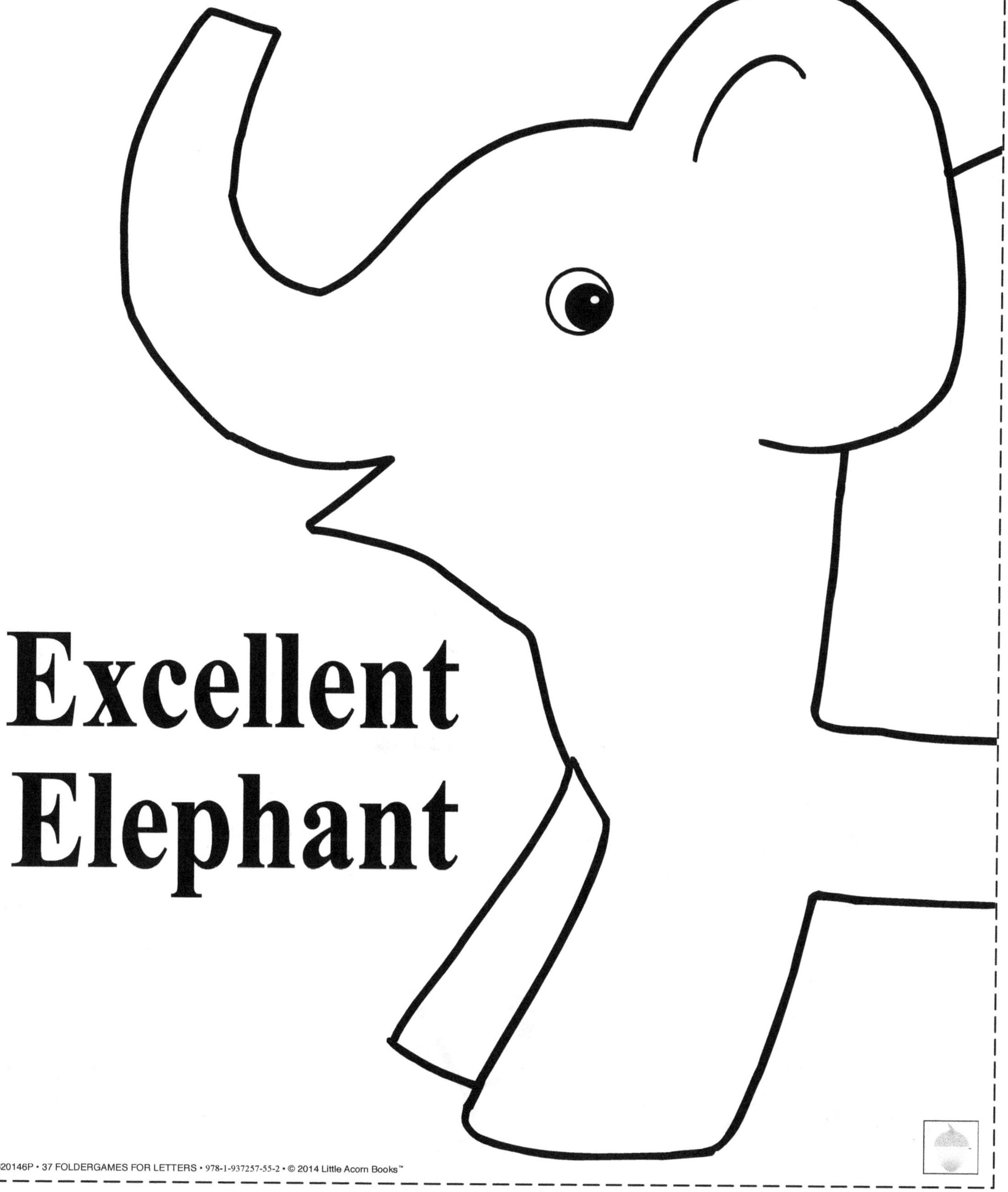

Dot-to-Dot

Excellent Elephant

Excellent Elephant
Sequencing Letters A-Z

Dot-to-Dot

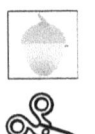

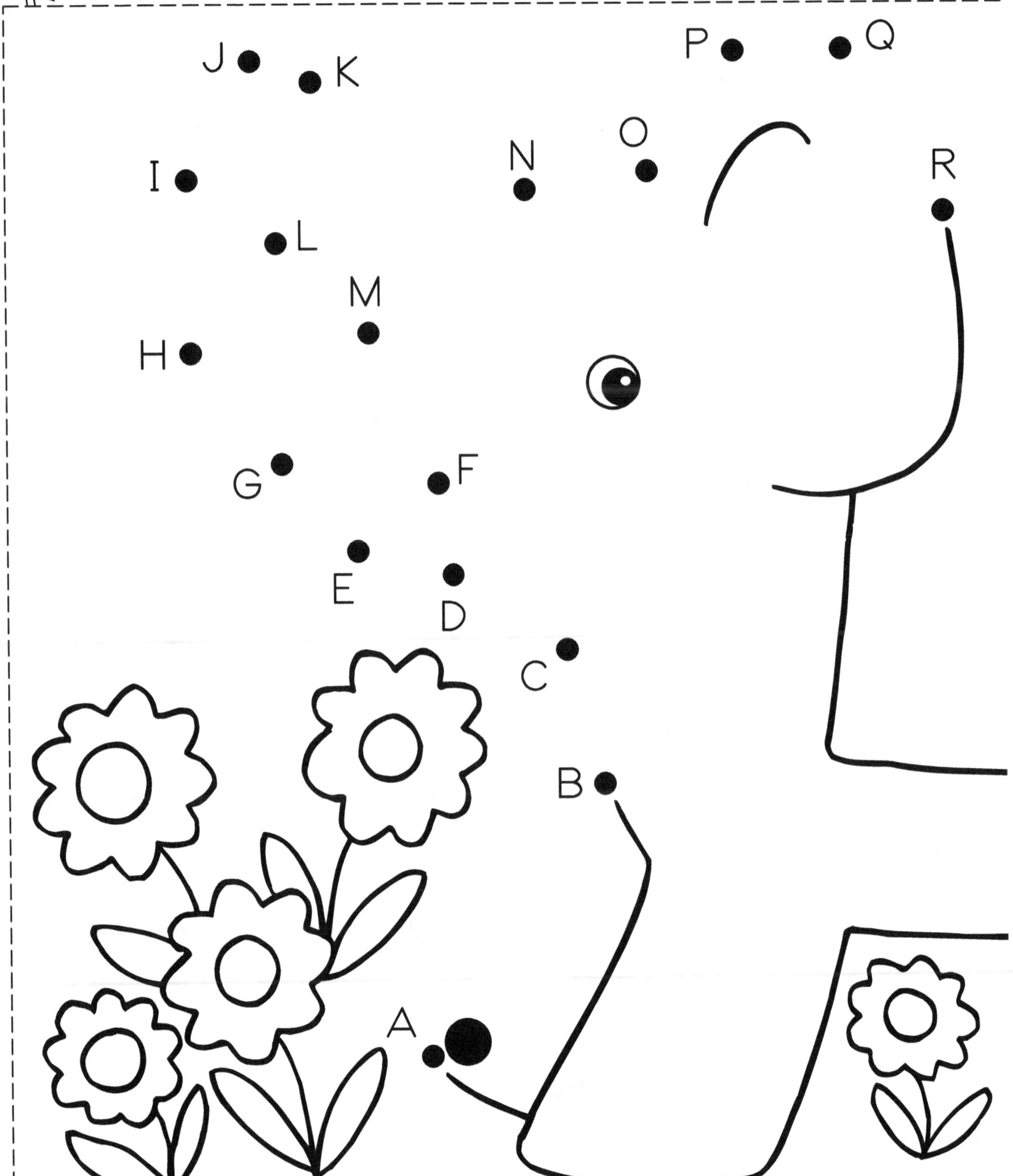

Excellent Elephant
Sequencing Letters A-Z

Dot-to-Dot

Start at the letter A. Follow the alphabet to connect the dots.

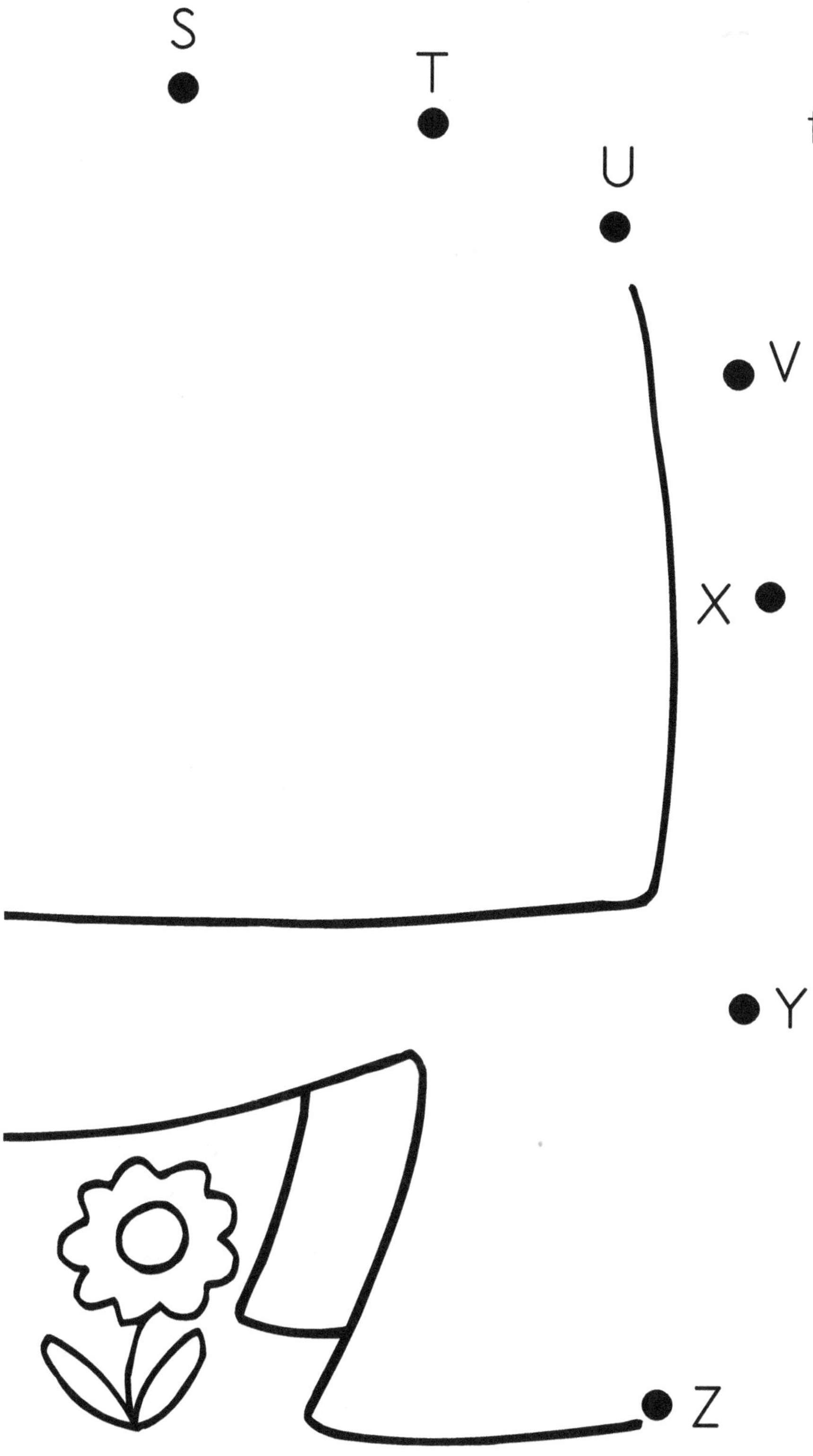

Excellent Elephant

Amazing Alligator
Sequencing Letters A-Z

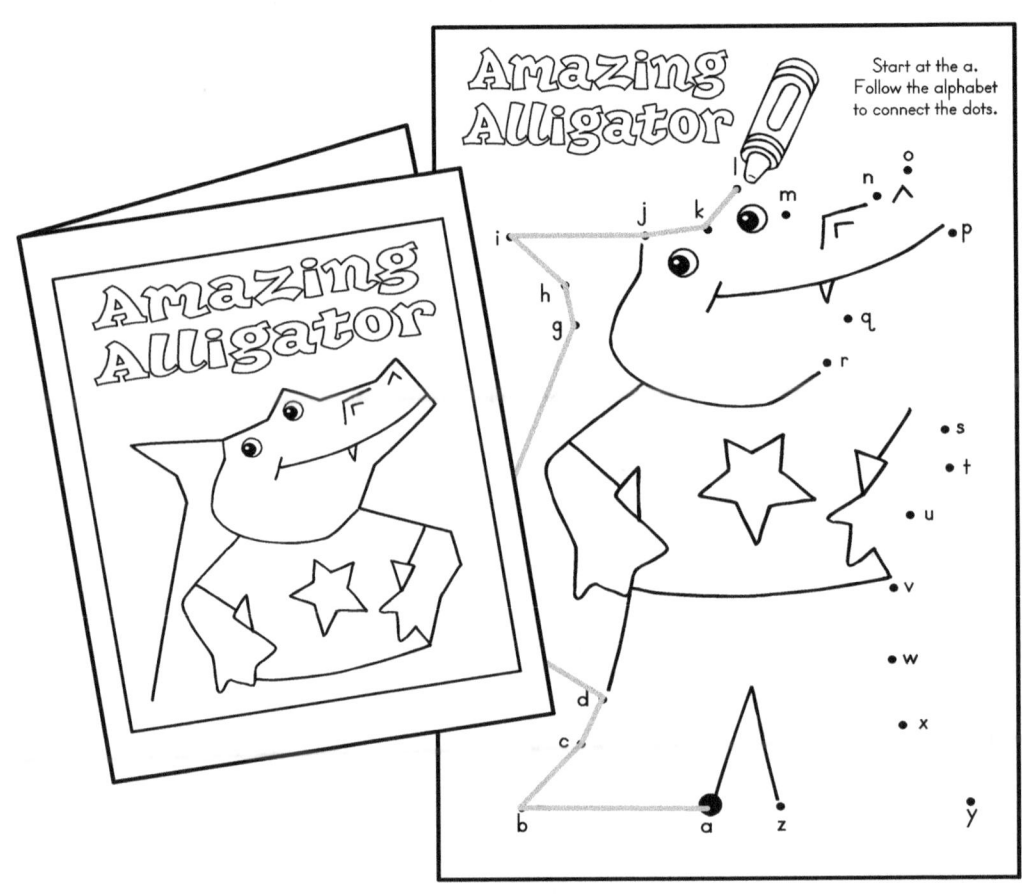

Assembly

Reproduce, cut out, and glue a set of oak tag handles (p. 192) to a standard-size file folder. Option: Decorate each handle with a copy of the alligators on this page. Reproduce, color, and cut out the "Amazing Alligator" patterns. Matching in the center, glue the dot-to-dot boards to the inside of the folder. Glue the cover art to the front of the folder, then laminate. Glue an envelope to the back of the folder to store a wipe-off marker or crayon and soft cloth. Option: Reproduce, cut out, and glue the Dot-to-Dot Playing Directions to the back of the folder.

Amazing Alligator Cover
Sequencing Letters A–Z
Dot-to-Dot

Amazing Alligator

Amazing Alligator
Sequencing Letters A-Z

Dot-to-Dot

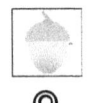

Start at the letter a. Follow the alphabet to connect the dots.

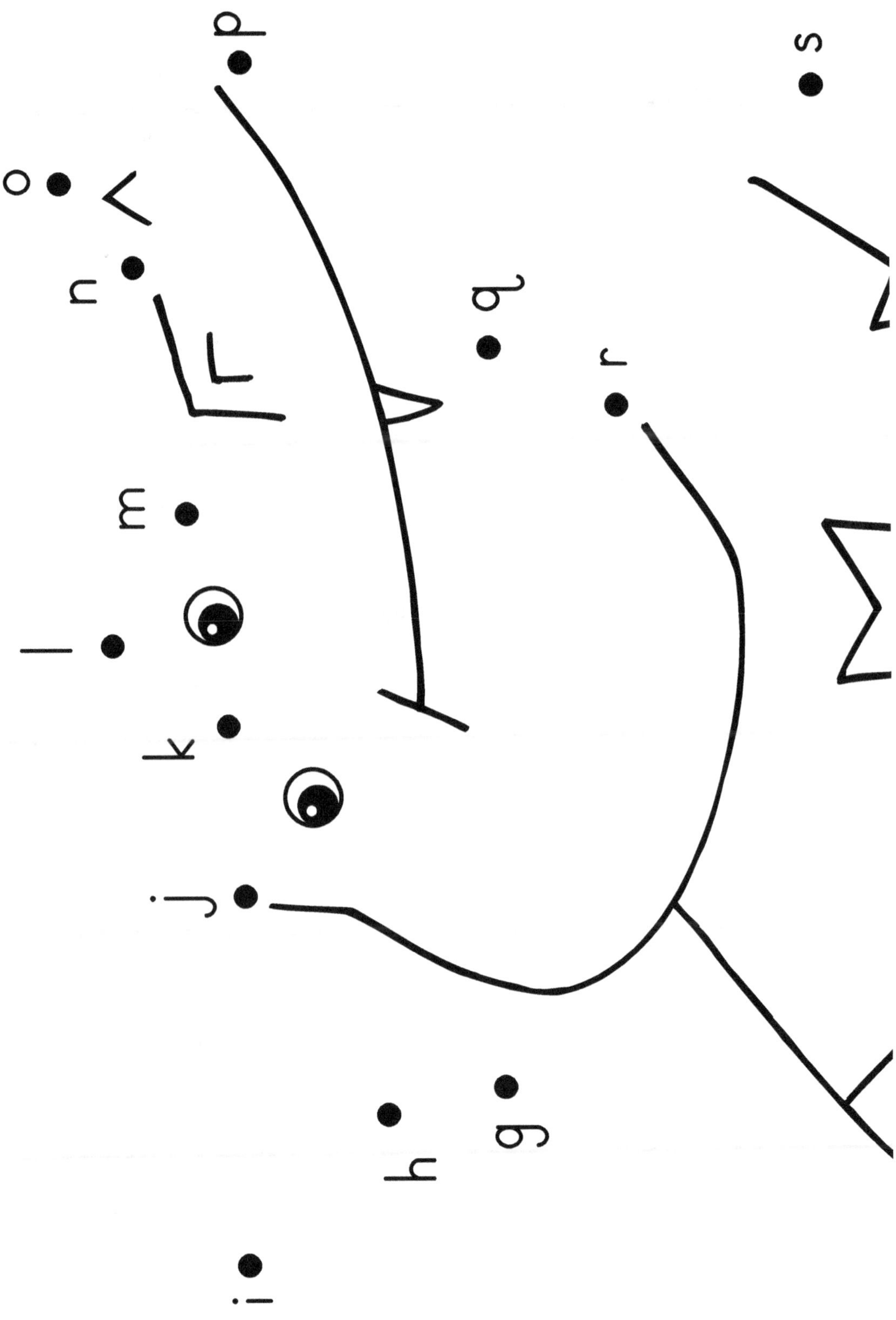

Amazing Alligator
Sequencing Letters A-Z

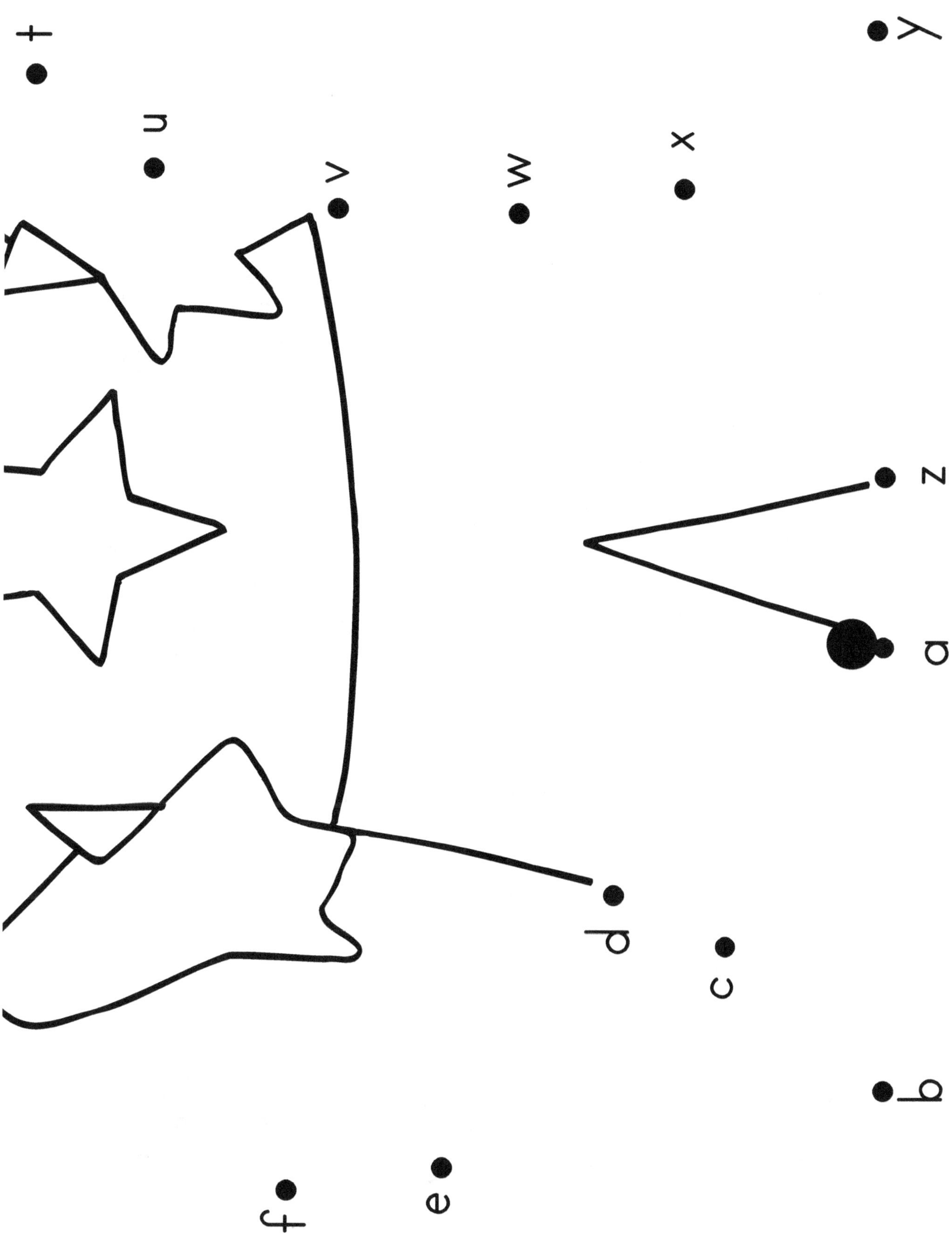

Dot-to-Dot

LAB20146P • 37 FOLDERGAMES FOR LETTERS • 978-1-937257-55-2 • © 2014 Little Acorn Books™

Ice Cream Scoops Lotto
Matching Pictures to Beginning Sound Letters A-F

Lotto

Assembly

Reproduce, cut out, and glue a set of oak tag handles (p. 192) to a standard-size file folder. Option: Decorate each handle with a copy of the ice cream cones shown above. Reproduce, color, and cut out the "Ice Cream Scoops Lotto" patterns. Glue the cover art to the front of the folder. Mount Lotto boards on colored construction paper, then laminate. Glue two envelopes to the inside of the folder for Lotto board, token, and card storage. Option: Reproduce, cut out, and glue the Lotto Playing Directions to the back of the folder. Note: Wipe-off markers or crayons can also be used to color in matches.

Tokens

Reproduce, color, and cut apart one set of cherry tokens for each player.

Ice Cream Scoops Lotto Cover
Matching Pictures to Beginning Sound Letters A-F

Lotto

Ice Cream Scoops Lotto

Ice Cream Scoops Lotto
Matching Pictures to Beginning Sound Letters A-F

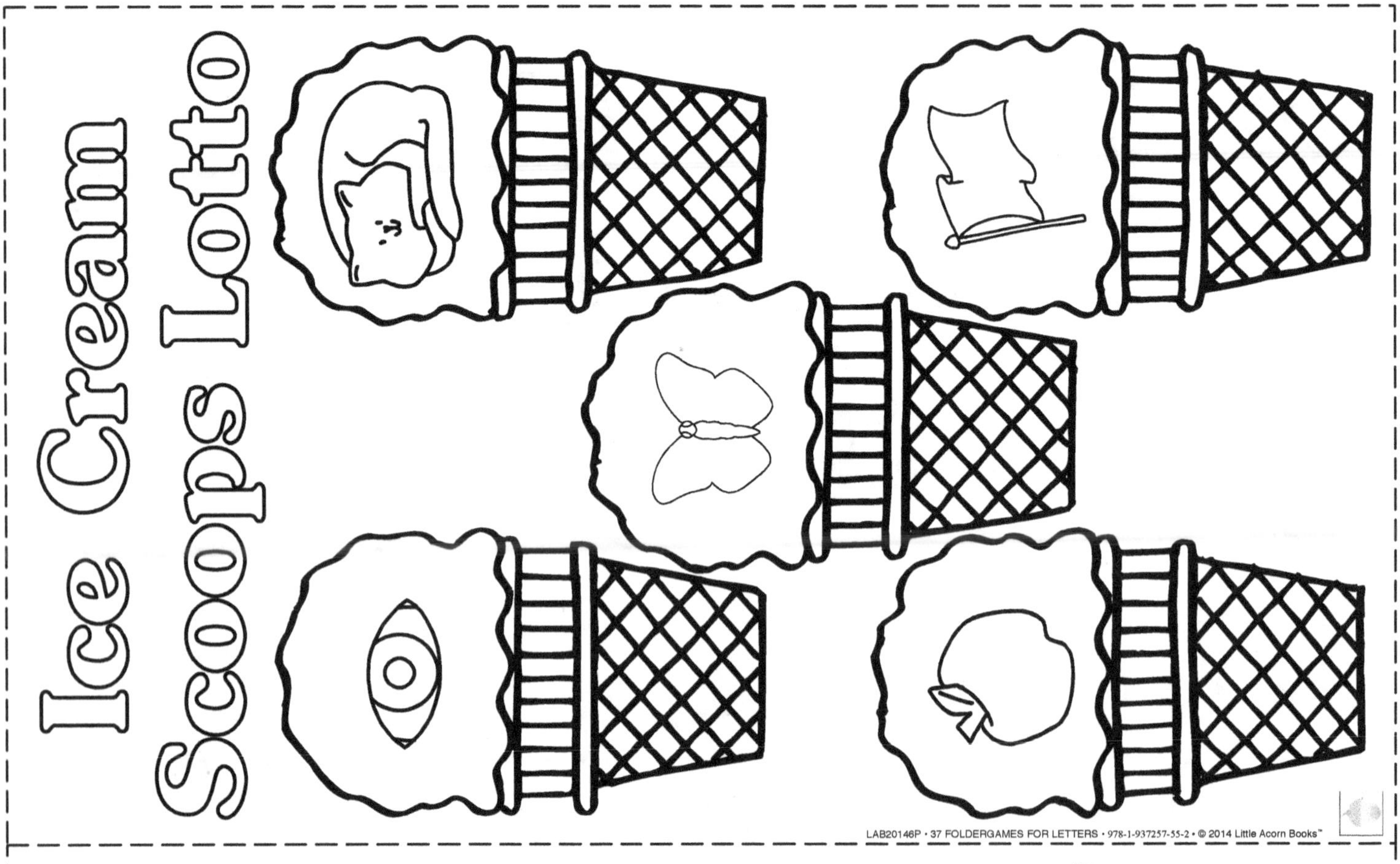

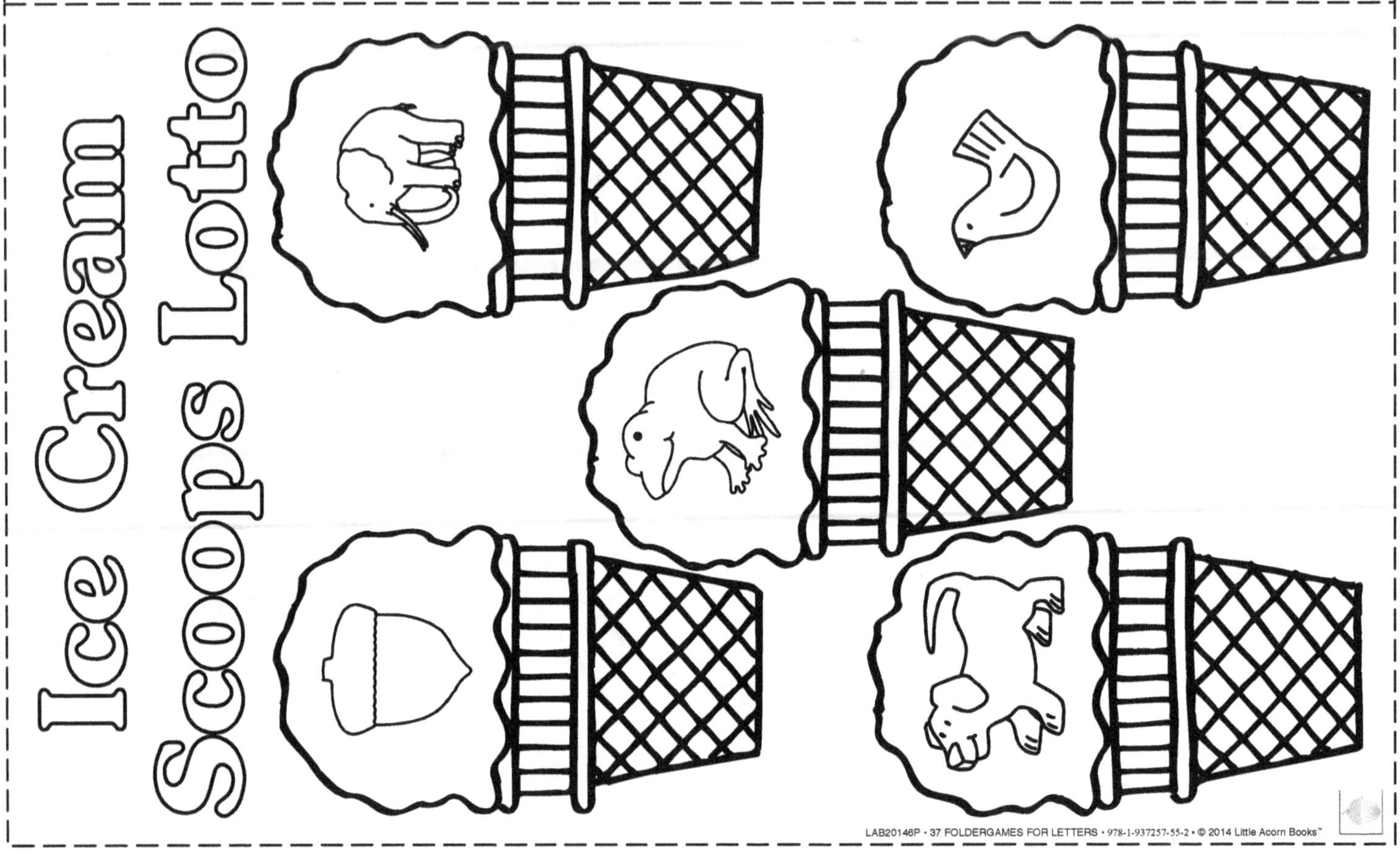

Ice Cream Scoops Lotto
Matching Pictures to Beginning Sound Letters A-F

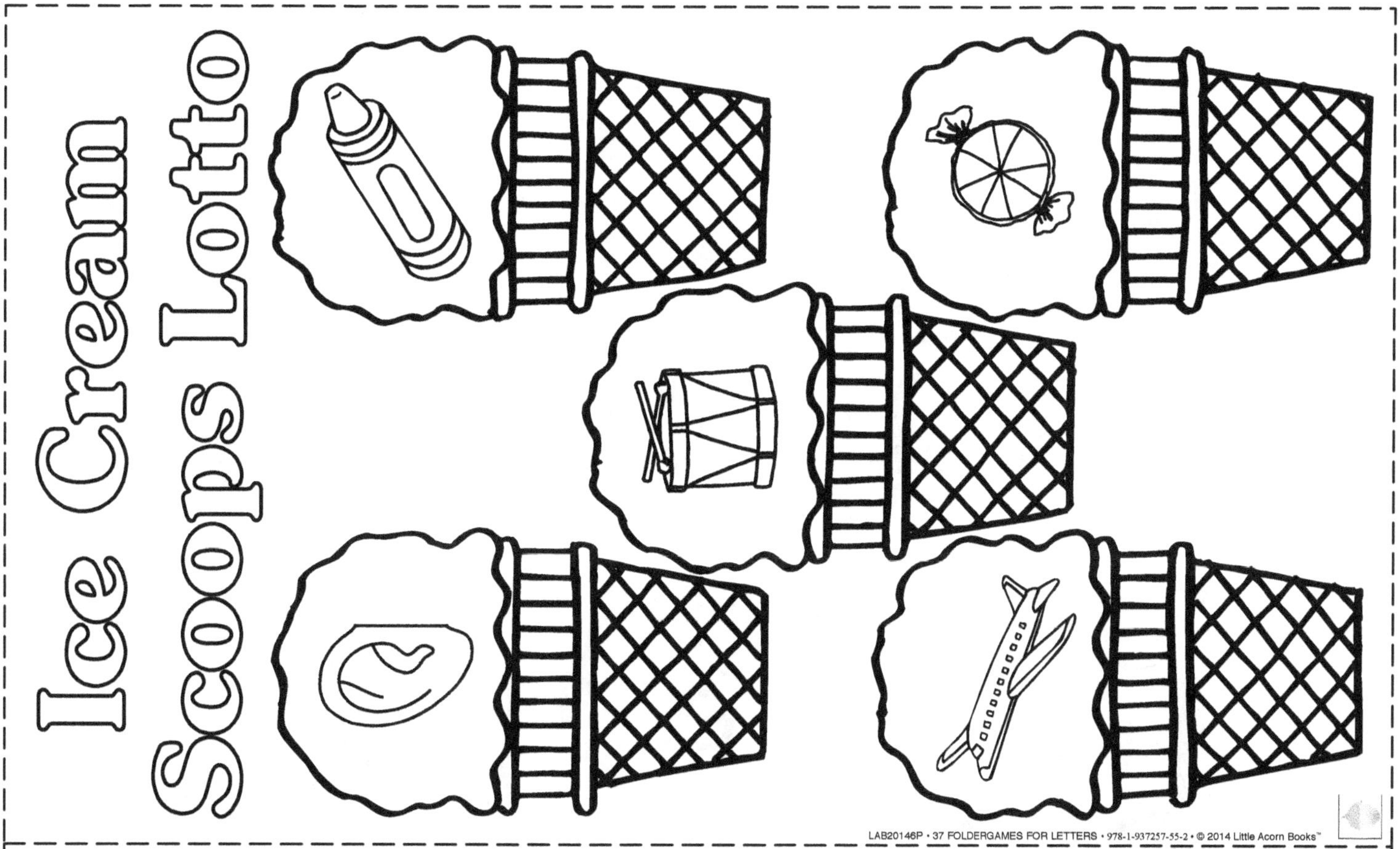

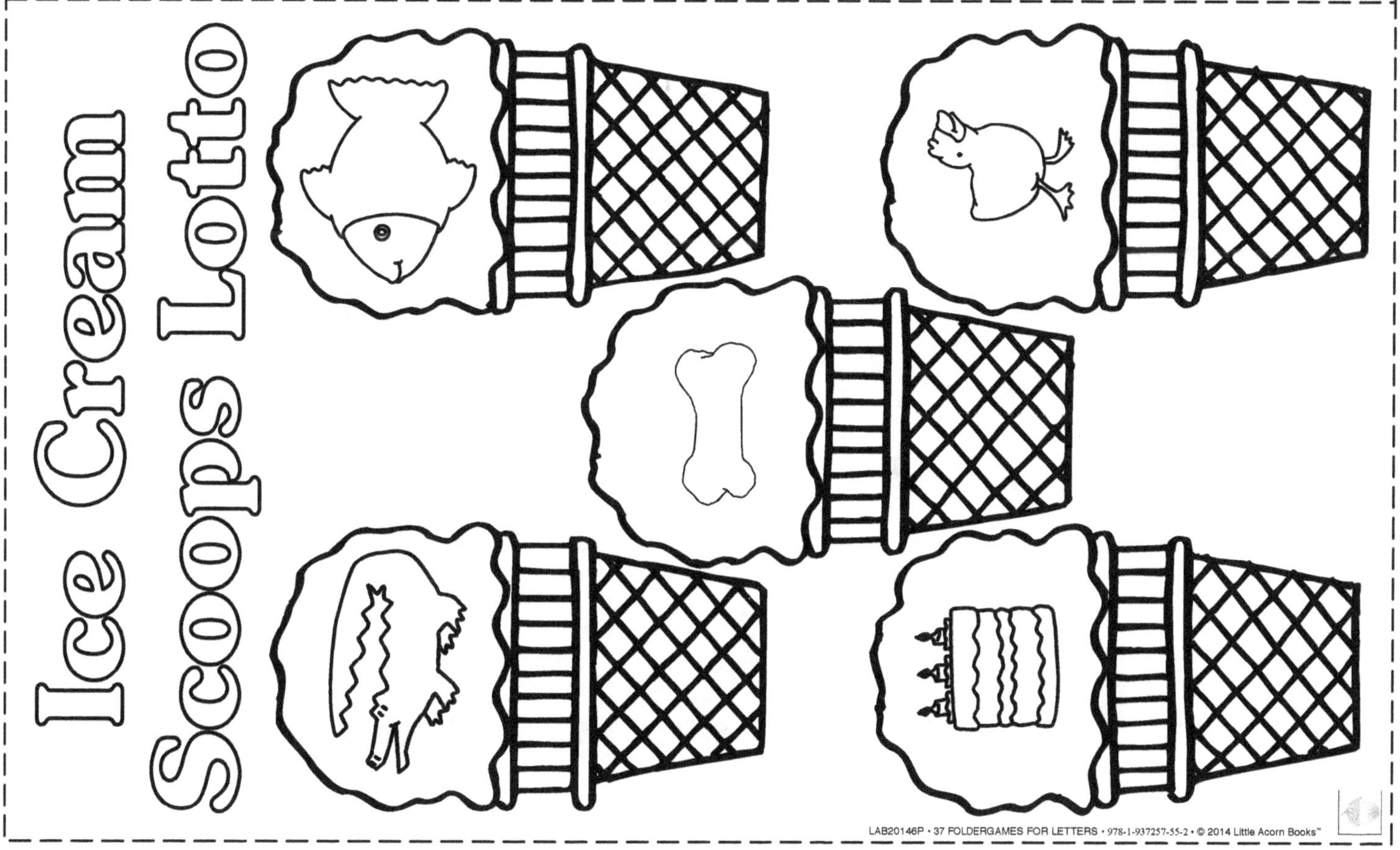

Lotto

Ice Cream Scoops Lotto
Matching Pictures to Beginning Sound Letters A-F

Lotto

Reproduce, color, and cut apart two sets of cards.

a	b	c
d	e	f
A	B	C
D	E	F

Candy Apples
Matching Pictures to Beginning Sound Letters F-K

Match Board

Assembly

Reproduce, cut out, and glue a set of oak tag handles (p. 192) to a standard-size file folder. Option: Decorate each handle with copies of the apples shown on this page. Reproduce, color, and cut out the "Candy Apples" patterns. Glue the match boards to the inside of the folder. Glue the cover art to the front of the folder. Decorate the border around the match board, then laminate. Reproduce, color, laminate, then cut apart three sets of game cards. Glue an envelope to the back of the folder for game card storage. Option: Reproduce, cut out, and glue the Match Board Playing Directions to the back of the folder.

Candy Apples Cover
Matching Pictures to Beginning Sound Letters F-K

Match Board

Candy Apples
Matching Pictures to Beginning Sound Letters F-K

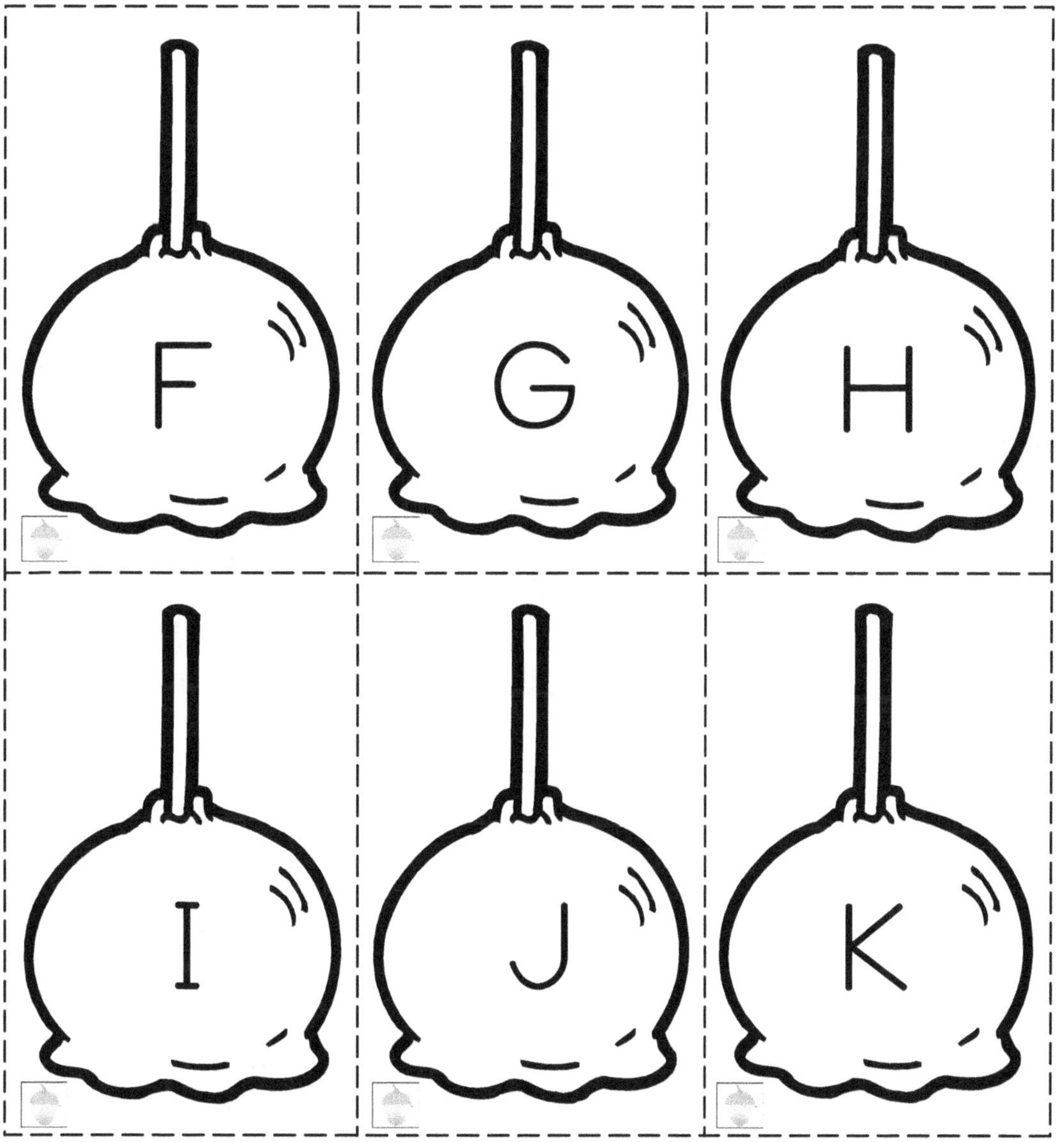

Match Board

F G H

I J K

Reproduce, color, and cut apart three sets of cards.

LAB20146P • 37 FOLDERGAMES FOR LETTERS • 978-1-937257-55-2 • © 2014 Little Acorn Books™   95

Candy Apples

Matching Pictures to Beginning Sound Letters F-K

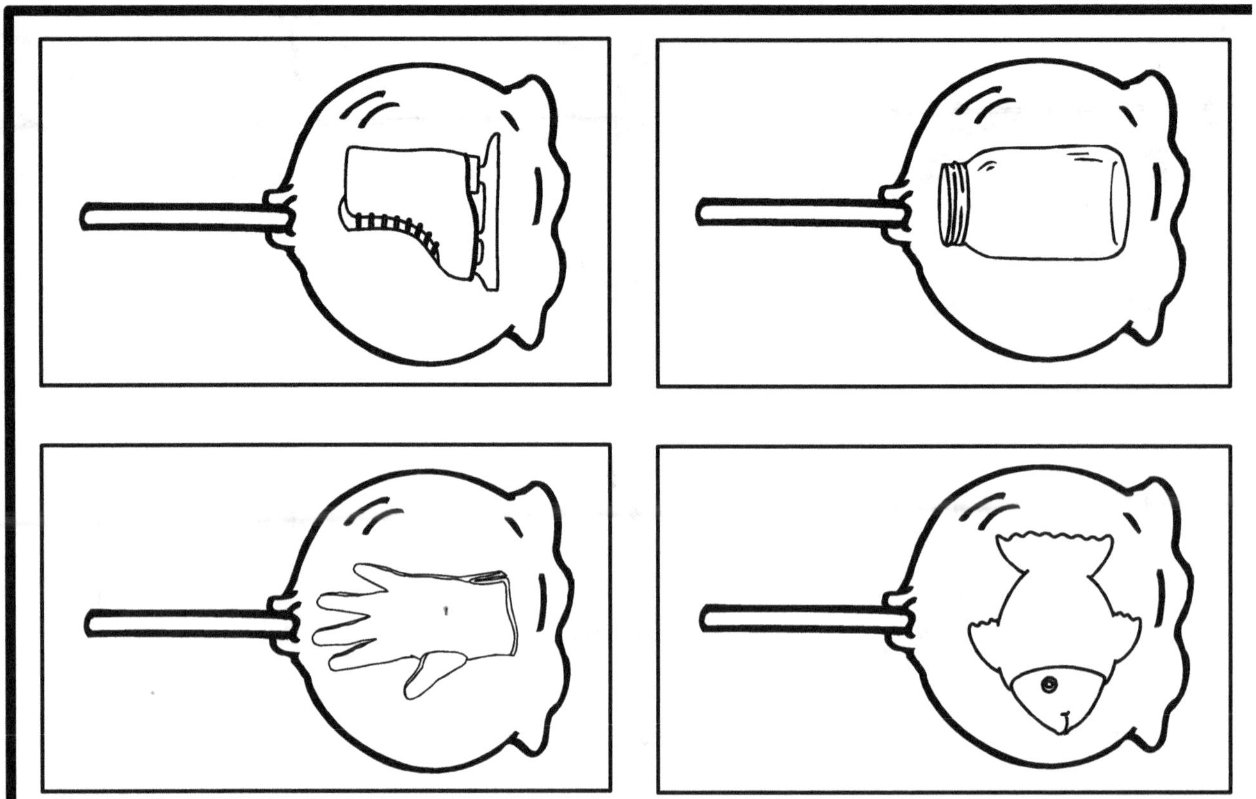

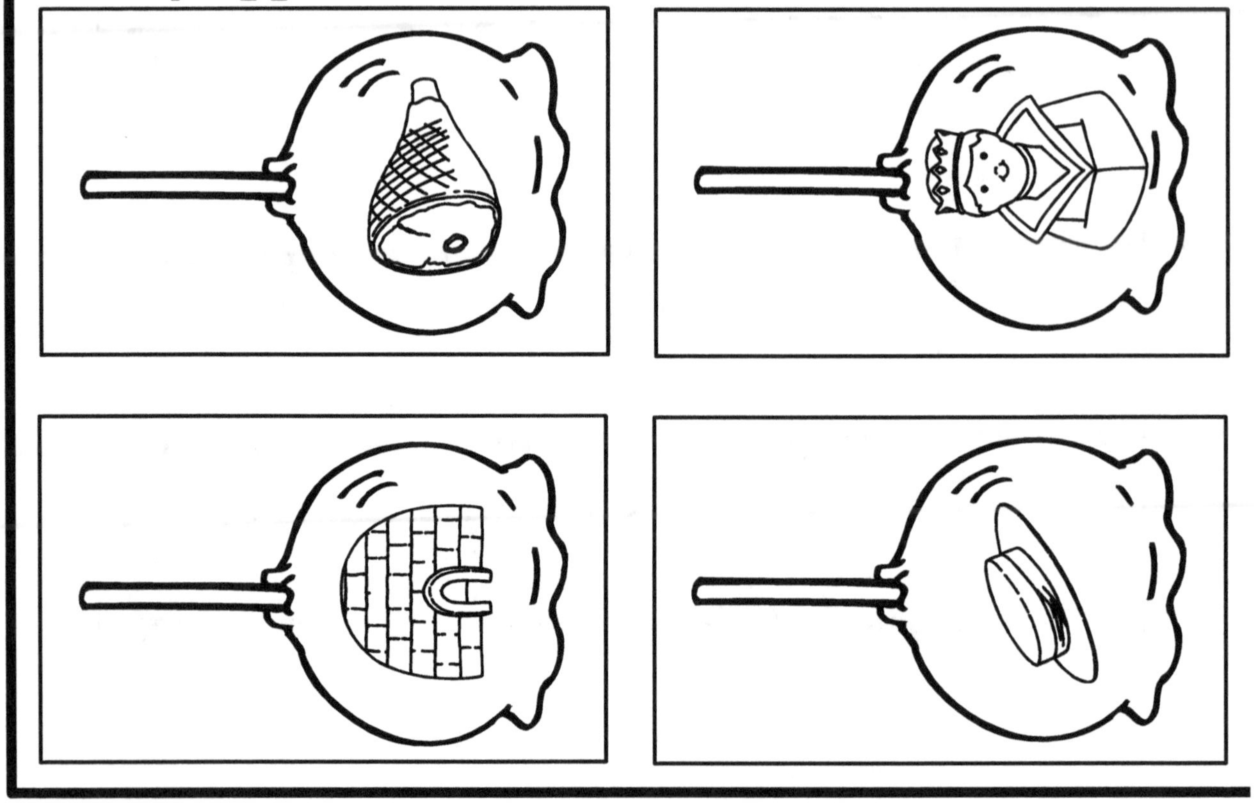

Match Board

Candy Apples

Candy Apples
Matching Pictures to Beginning Sound Letters F-K

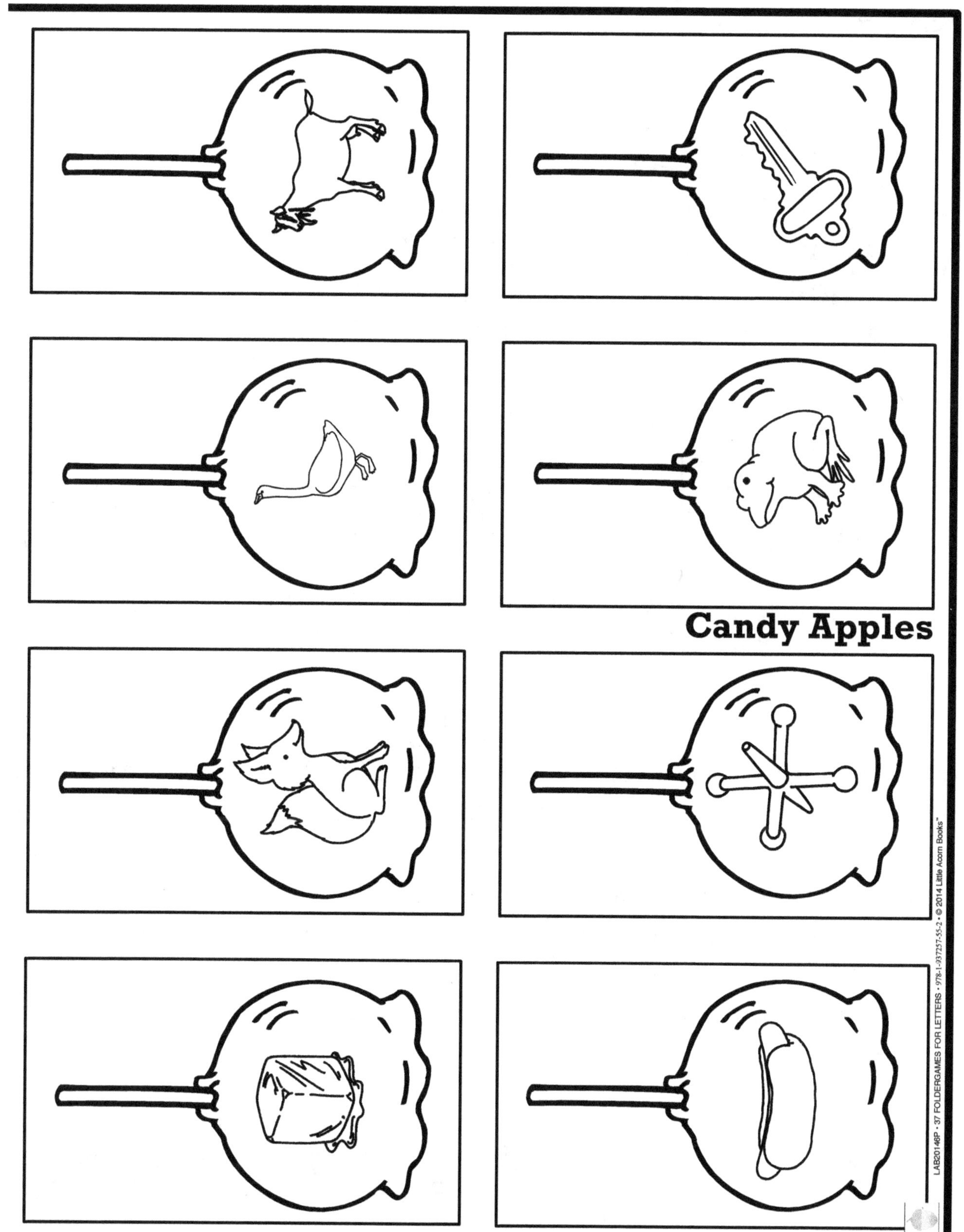

Match Board

Candy Apples

Circus Peanut Dominoes

Matching Pictures to Beginning Sound Letters K-P

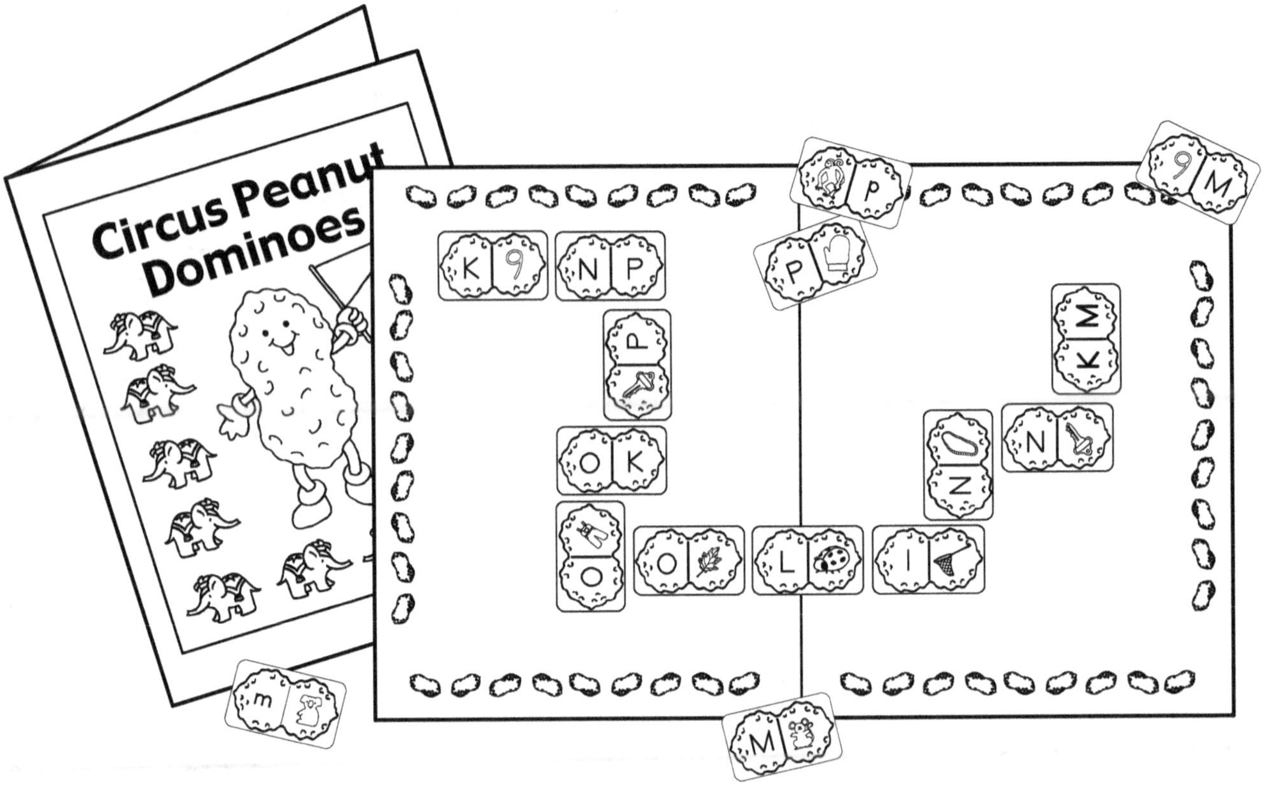

Dominoes

Assembly

Reproduce, cut out, and glue a set of oak tag handles (p. 192) to a standard-size file folder. Option: Decorate the handles with copies of the peanuts shown on this page. Reproduce, color, and cut out the "Circus Peanut Dominoes" patterns. Make extra sets of dominoes to accommodate more players. Glue the cover art to the front of the folder. Decorate the inside of the folder, then laminate. Reproduce, color, laminate, then cut apart the dominoes. Glue an envelope to the back of the folder to store dominoes. Option: Reproduce, cut out, and glue the Dominoes Playing Directions to the back of the folder.

Circus Peanut Dominoes Cover
Matching Pictures to Beginning Sound Letters K-P

Dominoes

Circus Peanut Dominoes

Circus Peanut Dominoes
Matching Pictures to Beginning Sound Letters K-P

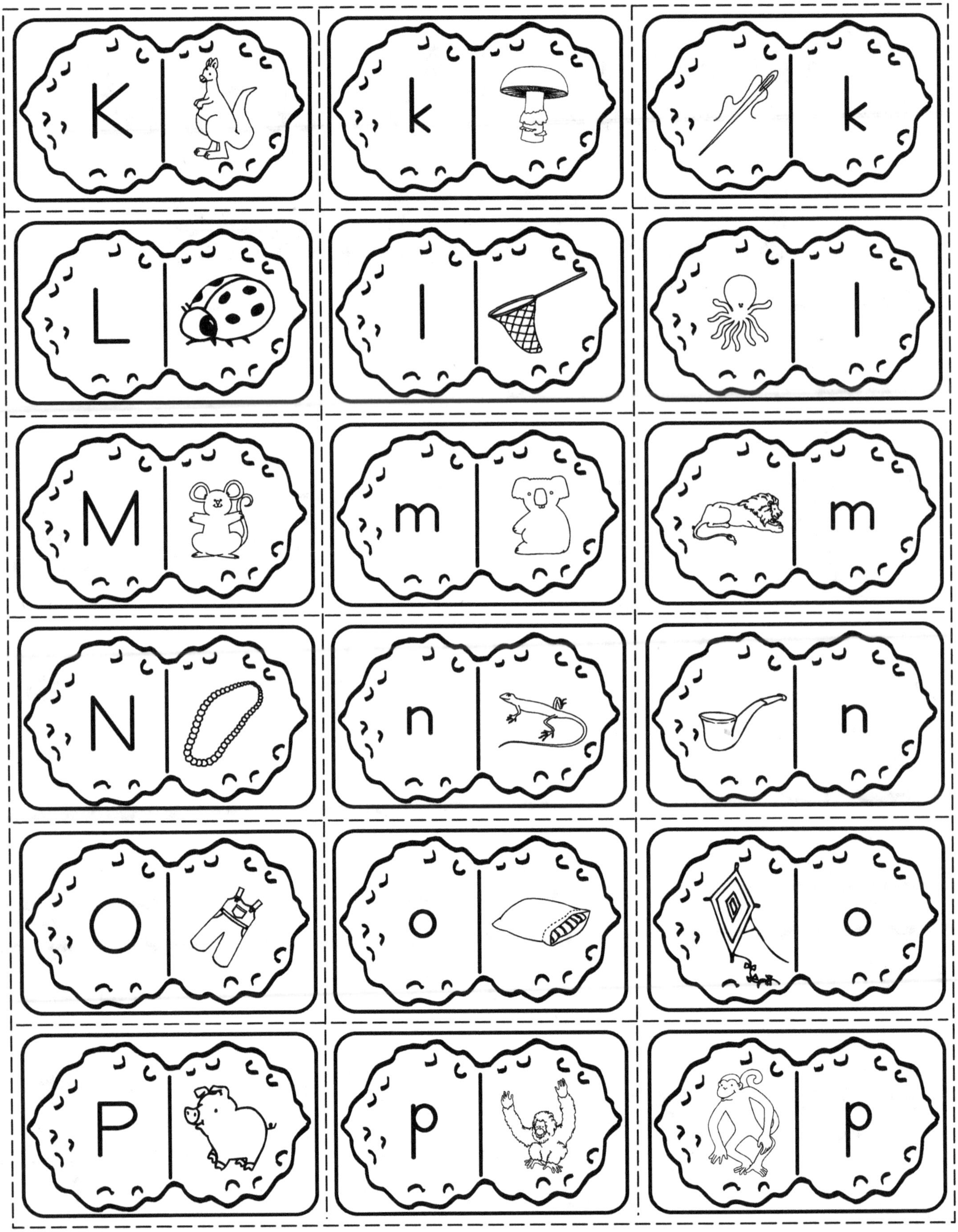

Dominoes

100 LAB20146P • 37 FOLDERGAMES FOR LETTERS • 978-1-937257-55-2 • © 2014 Little Acorn Books™

Circus Peanut Dominoes
Matching Pictures to Beginning Sound Letters K-P

Dominoes

Bats in the Attic

Matching Pictures to Beginning Sound Letters P-U

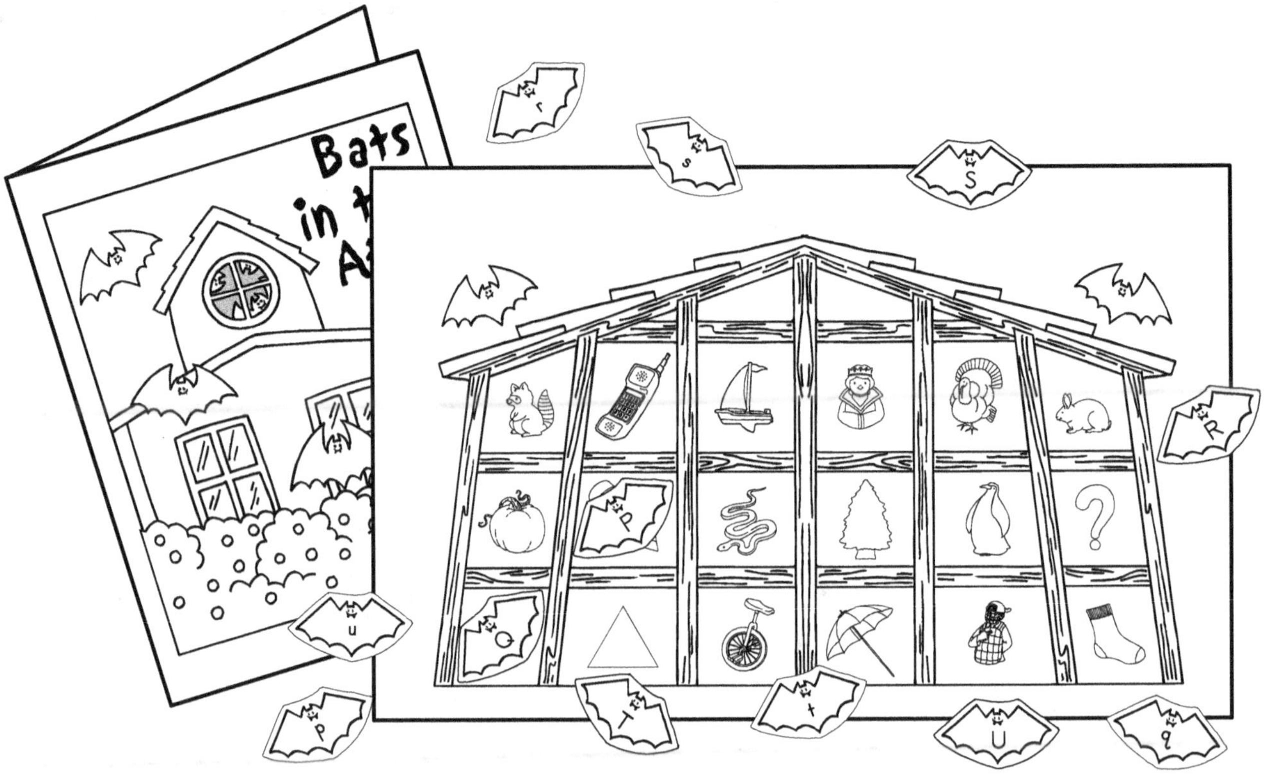

Match Board

Assembly

Reproduce, cut out, and glue a set of oak tag handles (p. 192) to a standard-size file folder. Option: Decorate each handle with copies of the bats shown on this page. Reproduce, color, and cut out the "Bats in the Attic" patterns. Glue the match boards to the inside of the folder. Glue the cover art to the front of the folder. Decorate the border around the match board, then laminate. Reproduce, color, laminate, then cut apart two sets of game cards. Glue an envelope to the back of the folder for game card storage. Option: Reproduce, cut out, and glue the Match Board Playing Directions to the back of the folder.

Bats in the Attic Cover
Matching Pictures to Beginning Sound Letters P-U

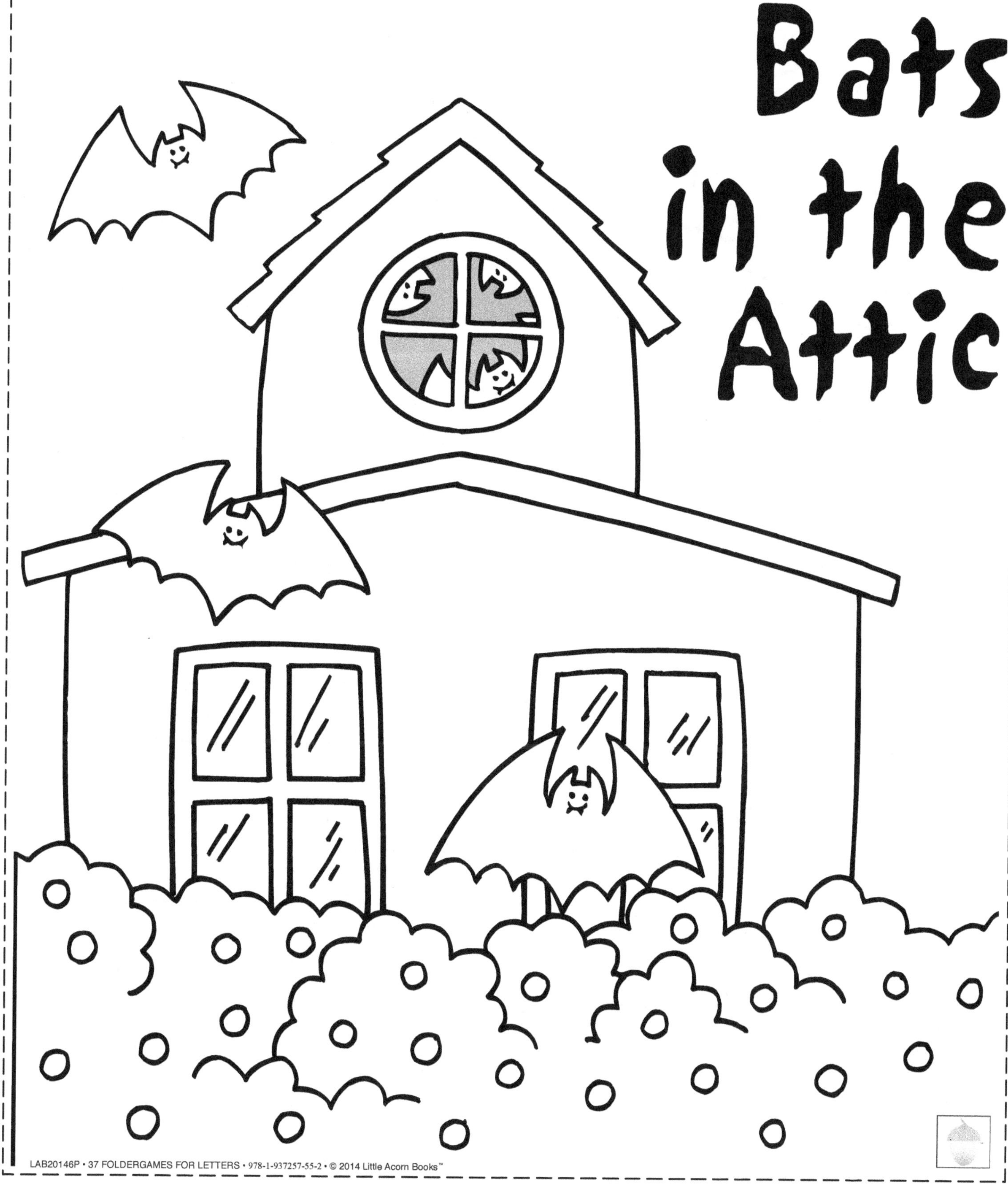

Match Board

Bats in the Attic

Bats in the Attic
Matching Pictures to Beginning Sound Letters P-U

Match Board

Look at each picture. Place a matching beginning sound letter bat on each picture.

Bats in the Attic

Matching Pictures to Beginning Sound Letters P-U

Match Board

Bats in the Attic
Matching Pictures to Beginning Sound Letters P-U

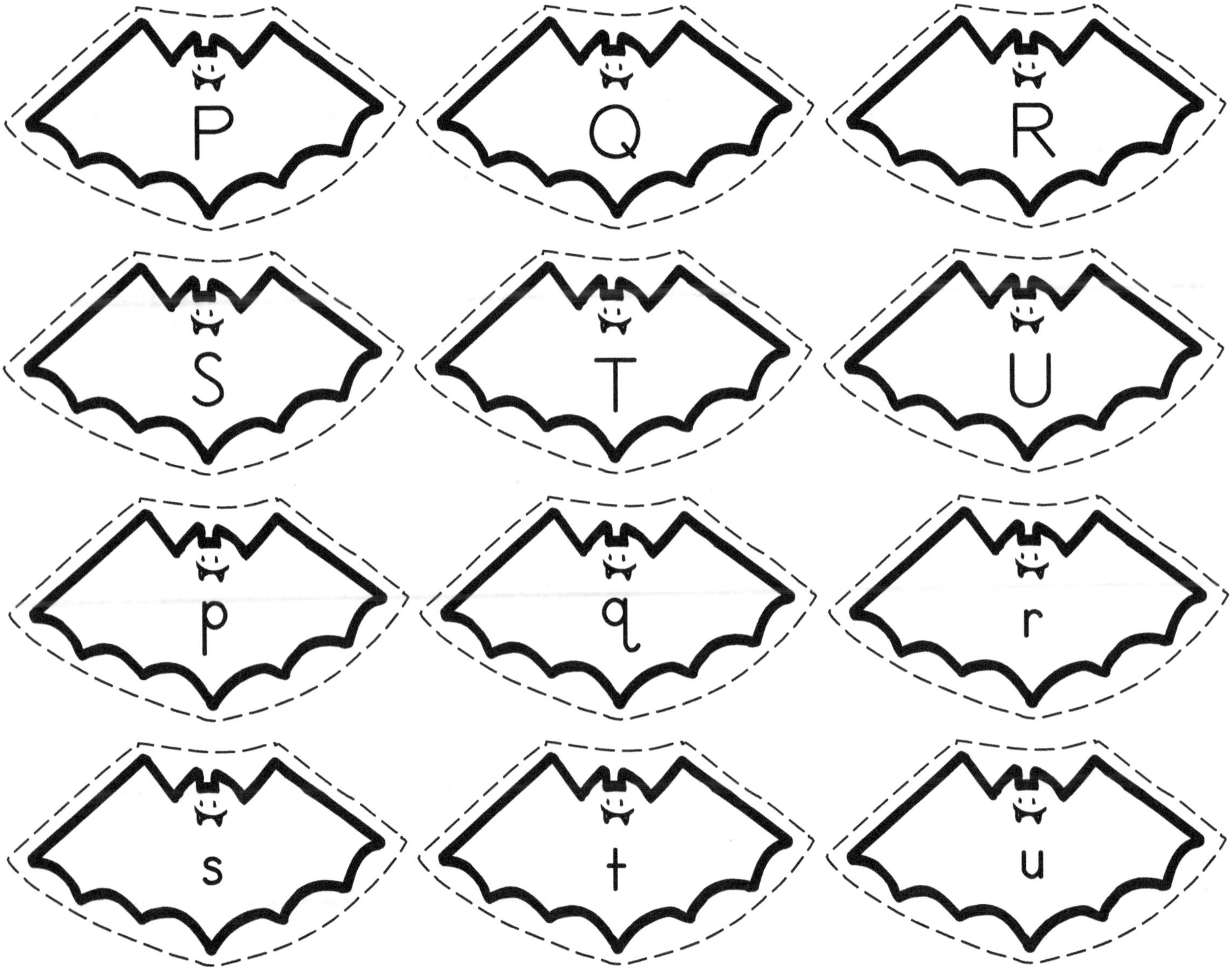

Match Board

P Q R

S T U

p q r

s t u

Reproduce, color, and cut out, two sets of bats.

Puppy Paws
Matching Pictures to Beginning Sound Letters U-Z

Clothespin Wheel

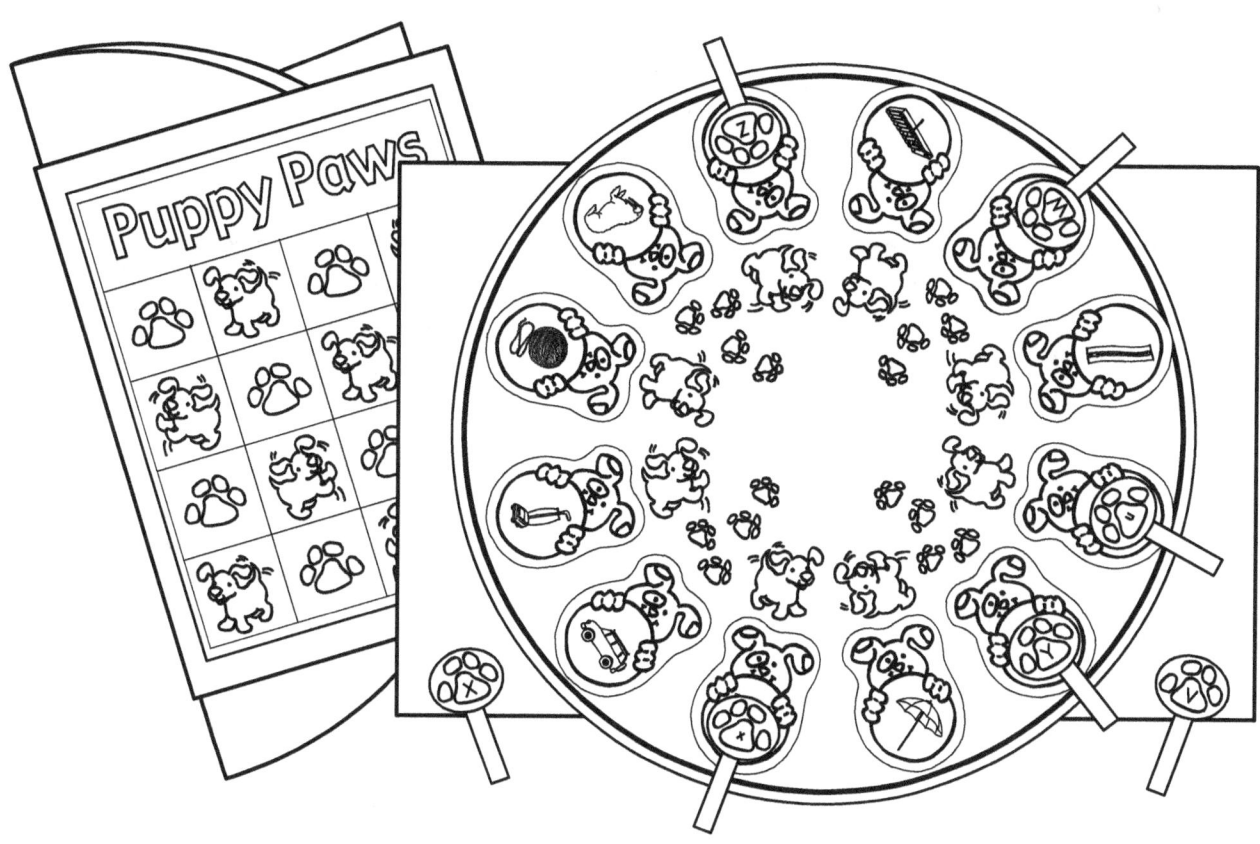

Assembly

Reproduce, cut out, and glue a set of oak tag handles (p. 192) to a standard-size file folder. Option: Decorate the handles with copies of the paw prints shown on this page. Reproduce, color, and cut out the "Puppy Paws" patterns. Glue the cover art to the front of the folder. Staple a resealable plastic bag to the back of the folder for clothespin storage. Glue the paw prints on clothespins. Meeting along the straight edges, glue the wheel quarters on a large poster board circle. Glue the wheel inside the folder, then glue the programmed puppies on the wheel. Option: Reproduce, cut out, and glue the Clothespin Wheel directions to the back of the folder.

Puppy Paws Cover
Matching Pictures to Beginning Sound Letters U-Z

Clothespin Wheel

Puppy Paws

Puppy Paws
Matching Pictures to Beginning Sound Letters U-Z

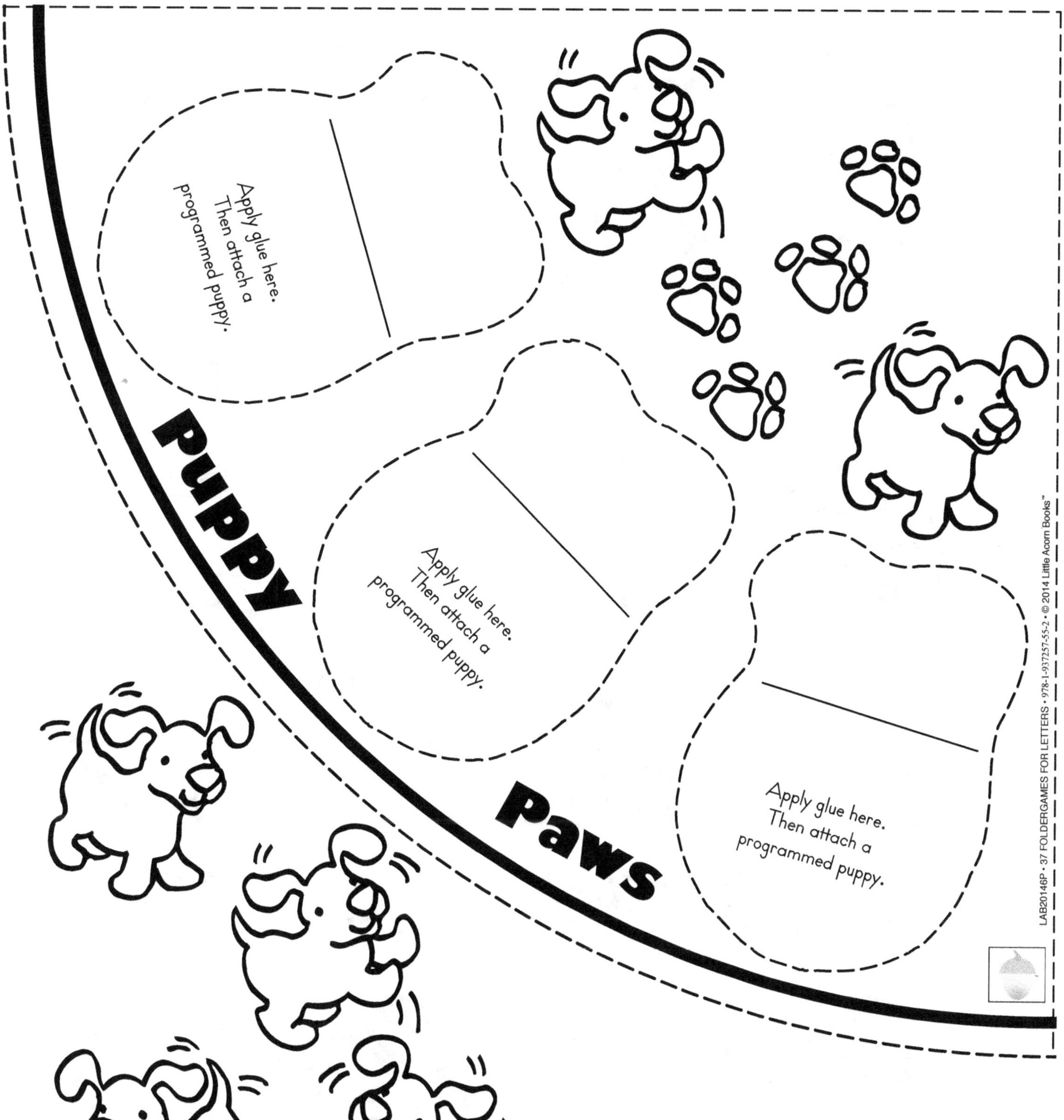

Clothespin Wheel

Apply glue here. Then attach a programmed puppy.

Apply glue here. Then attach a programmed puppy.

Apply glue here. Then attach a programmed puppy.

Puppy Paws

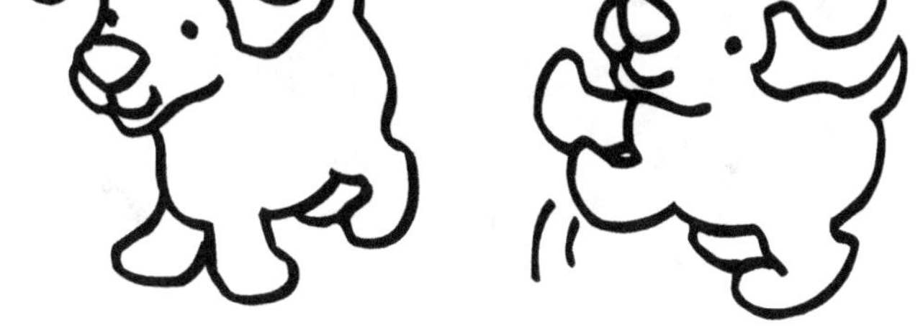

Reproduce, color, and cut out four wheel quarters. Meeting along the straight edges, glue the quarters on a large poster board circle.

Puppy Paws
Matching Pictures to Beginning Sound Letters U-Z

Clothespin Wheel

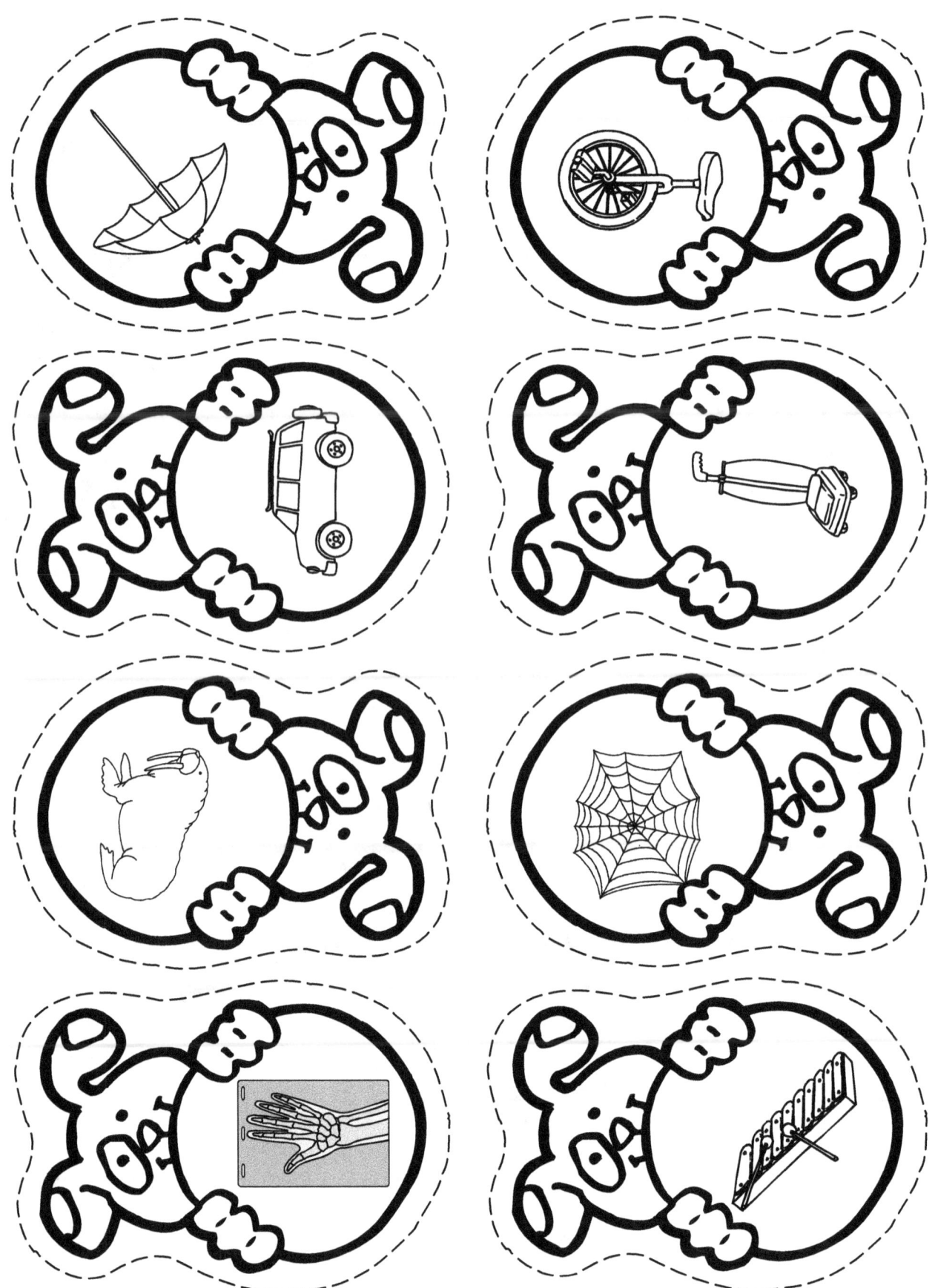

Reproduce and glue the puppies on the clothespin wheel. Do not glue down puppies' heads.

Puppy Paws
Matching Pictures to Beginning Sound Letters U-Z

Clothespin Wheel

Reproduce and glue the puppies on the clothespin wheel. Do not glue down puppies' heads.

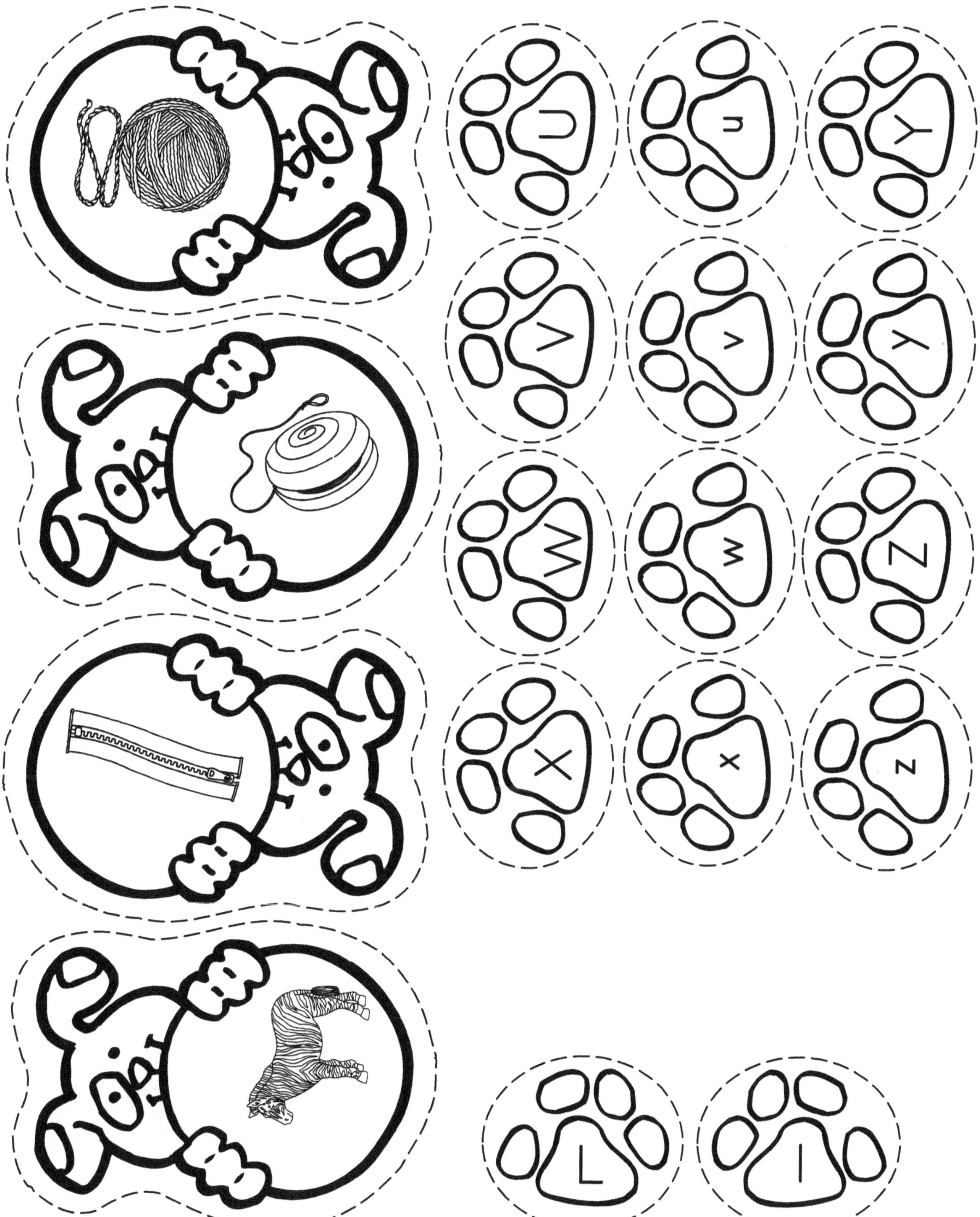

Follow the Rainbow
Matching Pictures to Ending Sound Letters A, B, D, E, F, G

Trail Game

Assembly

Reproduce, cut out, and glue a set of oak tag handles (p. 192) to a standard-size file folder. Option: Decorate each handle with a copy of the butterflies shown above. Reproduce, color, and cut out the "Follow the Rainbow" patterns. Matching in the center, glue the game board patterns to the inside of the folder. Glue the cover art to the front of the folder. Decorate the border around the game board, then laminate. Reproduce, color, laminate, then cut out the pawns and game cards. Glue an envelope to the back of the folder for pawn and game card storage. Option: Reproduce, cut out, and glue the Trail Game Playing Directions to the back of the folder.

Pawns

Follow the Rainbow Cover
Matching Pictures to Ending Sound Letters A, B, D, E, F, G

Trail Game

Follow the Rainbow

Follow the Rainbow
Matching Pictures to Ending Sound Letters A, B, D, E, F, G

Trail Game

Follow the Rainbow
Matching Pictures to Ending Sound Letters A, B, D, E, F, G

Trail Game

Help the butterflies find their way to the end of the rainbow.

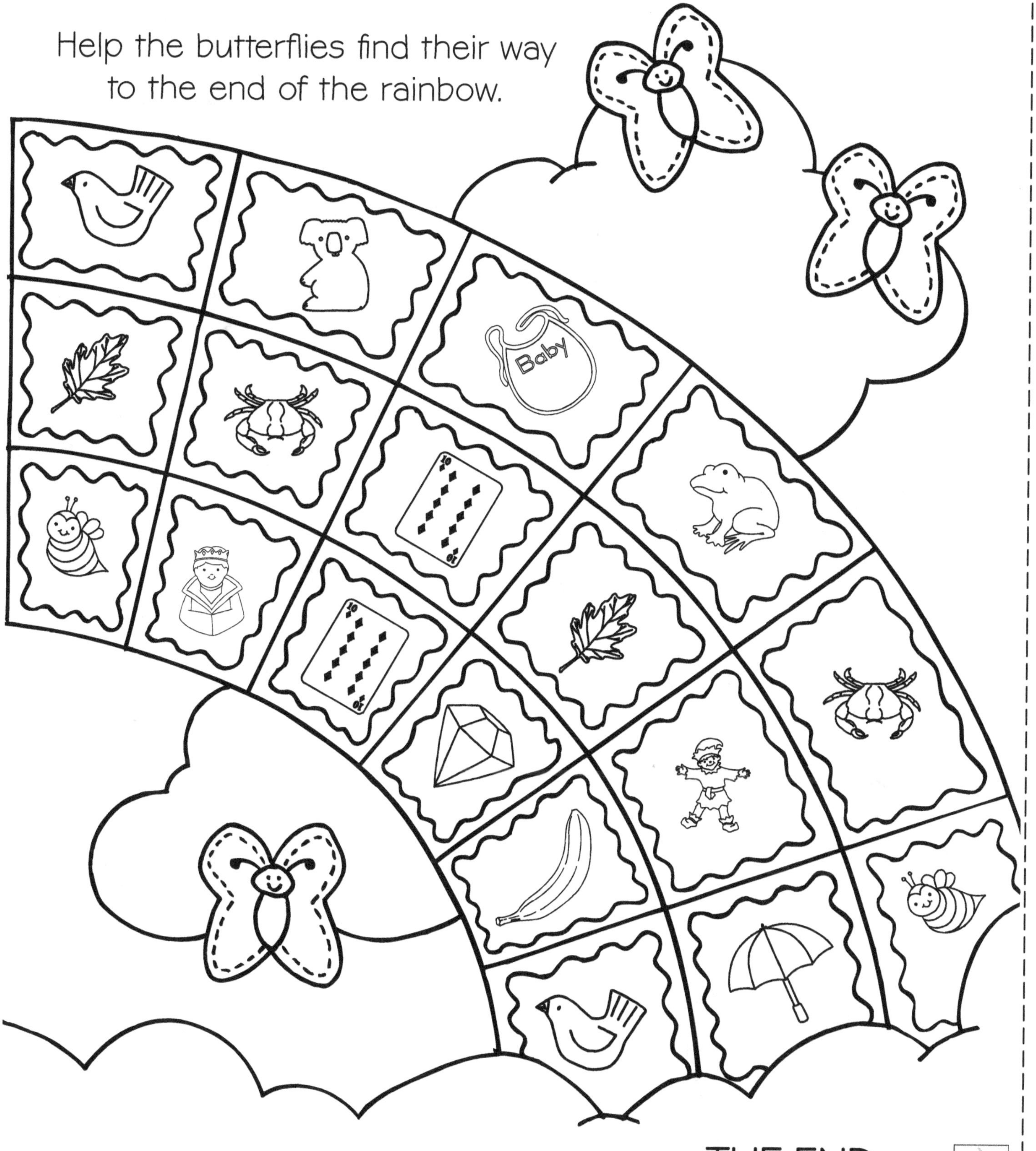

THE END

Follow the Rainbow
Matching Pictures to Ending Sound Letters A, B, D, E, F, G

Trail Game

a	a	a	e
b	b	b	e
d	d	d	e
f	f	f	e
	g	g	g

Reproduce, color, and cut apart the cards.

Hearts and Flowers

Matching Pictures to Ending Sound Letters G, K, L, M, N

Clothespin Match-ups

Assembly

Reproduce, cut out, and glue a set of oak tag handles (p. 192) to a standard-size file folder. Option: Decorate the handles with heart stickers or copies of the hearts shown on this page. Reproduce, color, and cut out the "Hearts and Flowers" patterns. Glue the flowers on clothespins. Glue two placement templates to the inside of the folder. Then glue six hearts to each template. Glue the cover art to the front of the folder. Staple a resealable plastic bag to the back of the folder for clothespin storage. Option: Reproduce, cut out, and glue the Clothespin Match-ups Playing Directions to the back of the folder.

Hearts and Flowers Cover — Clothespin Match-ups
Matching Pictures to Ending Sound Letters G, K, L, M, N

Hearts and Flowers

Matching Pictures to Ending Sound Letters G, K, L, M, N

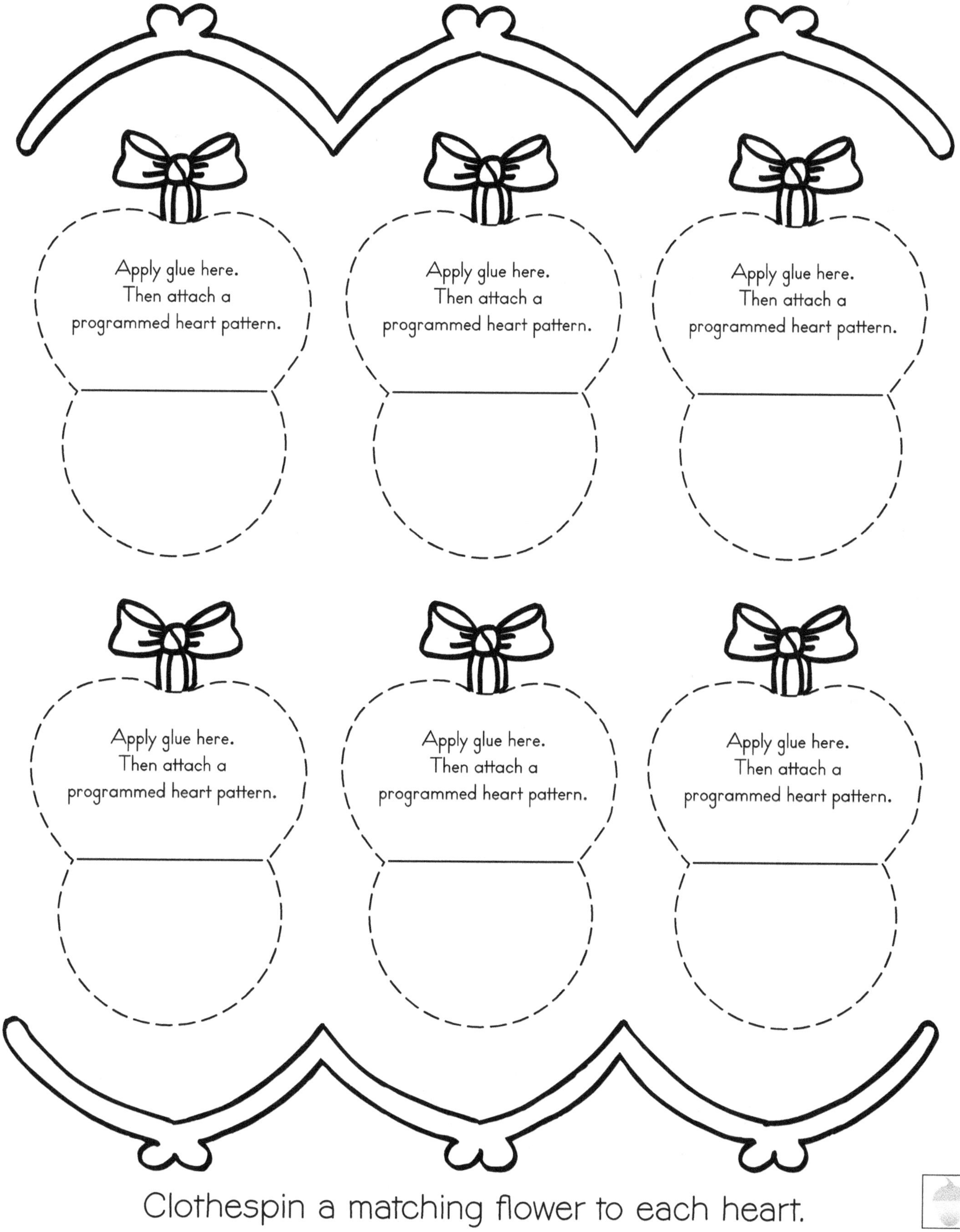

Clothespin Match-ups

Apply glue here. Then attach a programmed heart pattern.

Apply glue here. Then attach a programmed heart pattern.

Apply glue here. Then attach a programmed heart pattern.

Apply glue here. Then attach a programmed heart pattern.

Apply glue here. Then attach a programmed heart pattern.

Apply glue here. Then attach a programmed heart pattern.

Clothespin a matching flower to each heart.

LAB20146P • 37 FOLDERGAMES FOR LETTERS • 978-1-937257-55-2 • © 2014 Little Acorn Books™

Hearts and Flowers
Matching Pictures to Ending Sound Letters G, K, L, M, N

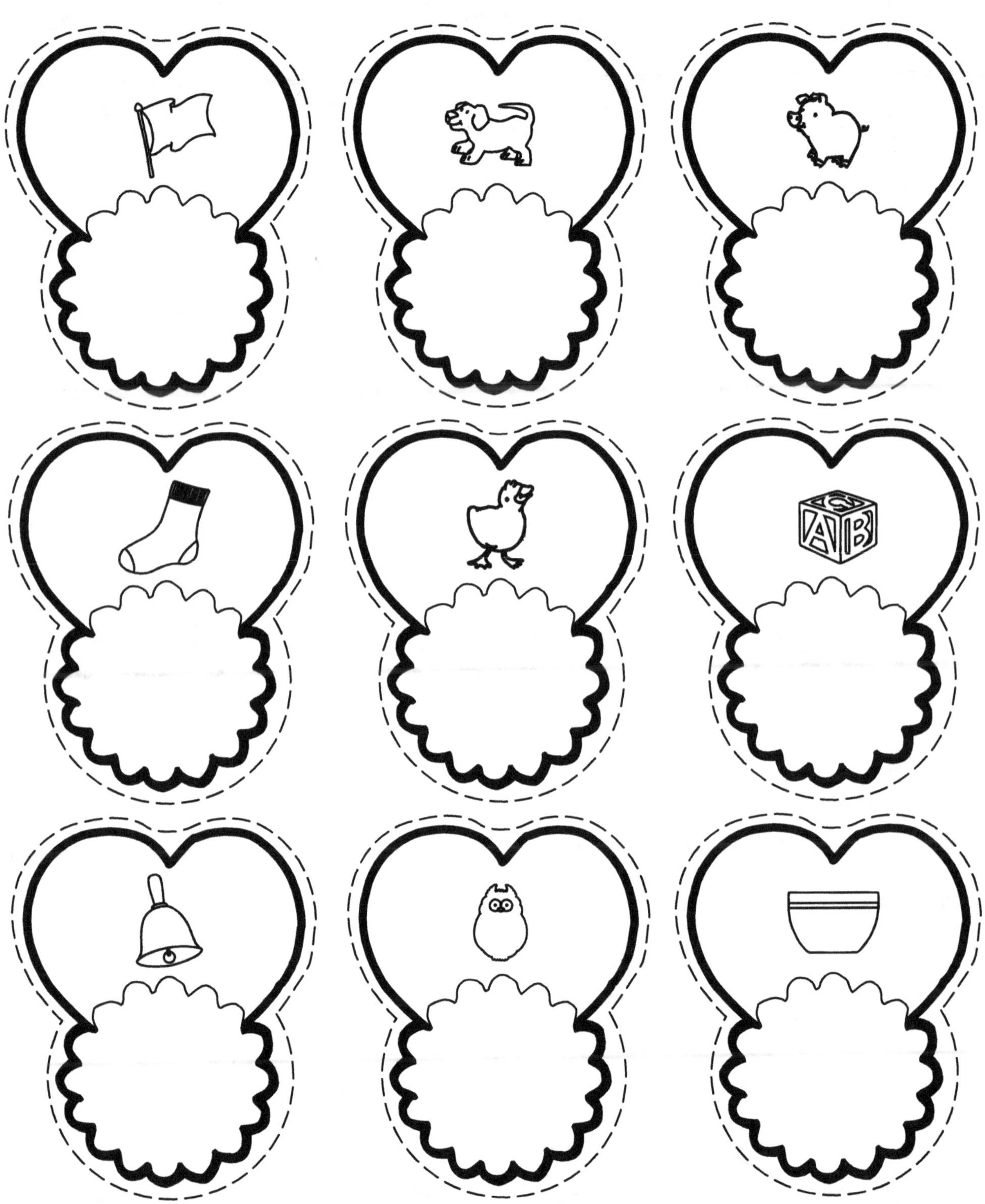

Clothespin Match-ups

Reproduce, color, cut out, then glue each heart on a placement template.
Do not glue down flowers.

Hearts and Flowers

Matching Pictures to Ending Sound Letters G, K, L, M, N

Clothespin Match-ups

Reproduce, color, cut out, then glue each heart on a placement template.
Do not glue down flowers.

Hearts and Flowers
Matching Pictures to Ending Sound Letters G, K, L, M, N

Clothespin Match-ups

Reproduce, color, cut out, and glue each flower on a clothespin.

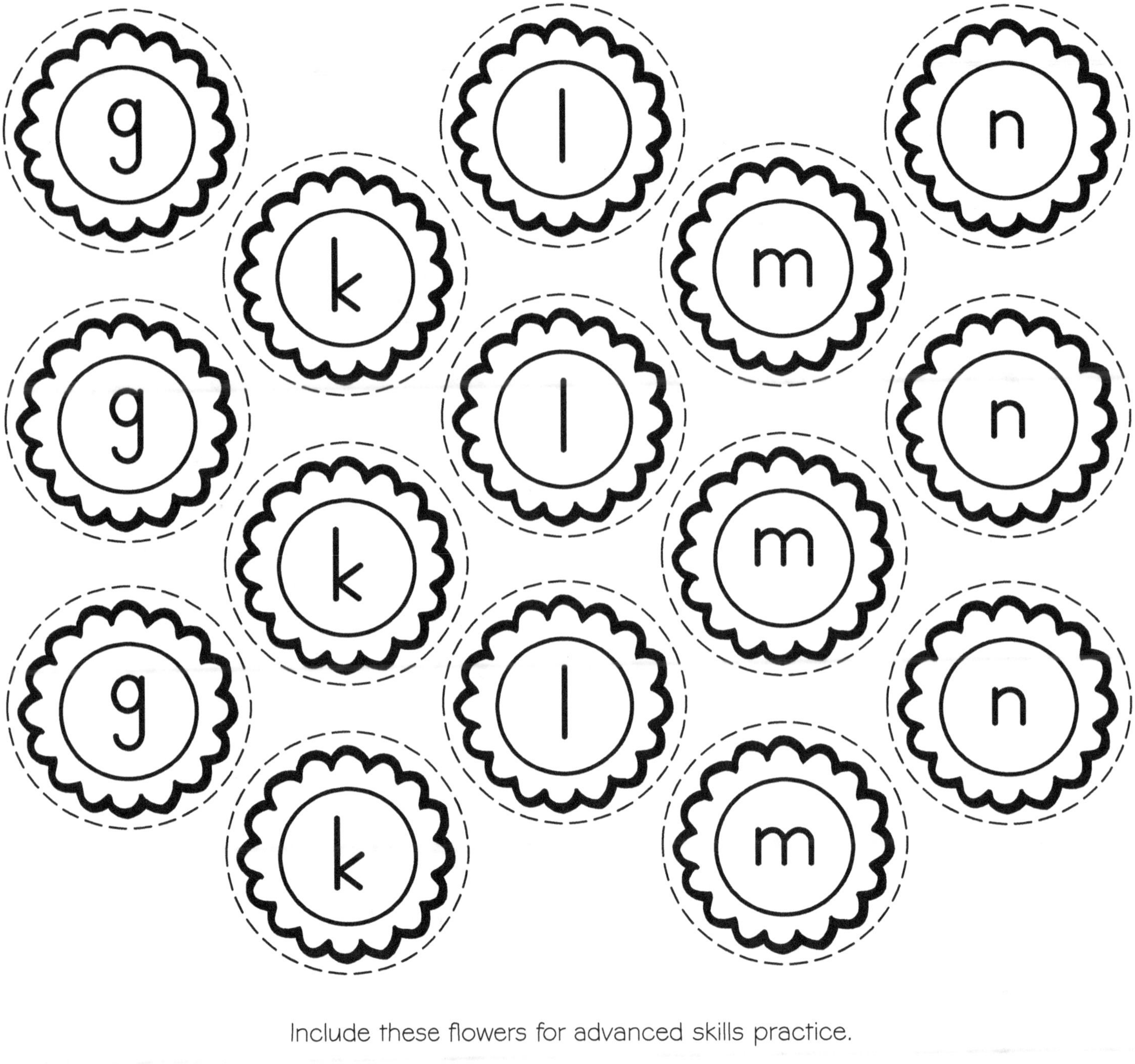

Include these flowers for advanced skills practice.

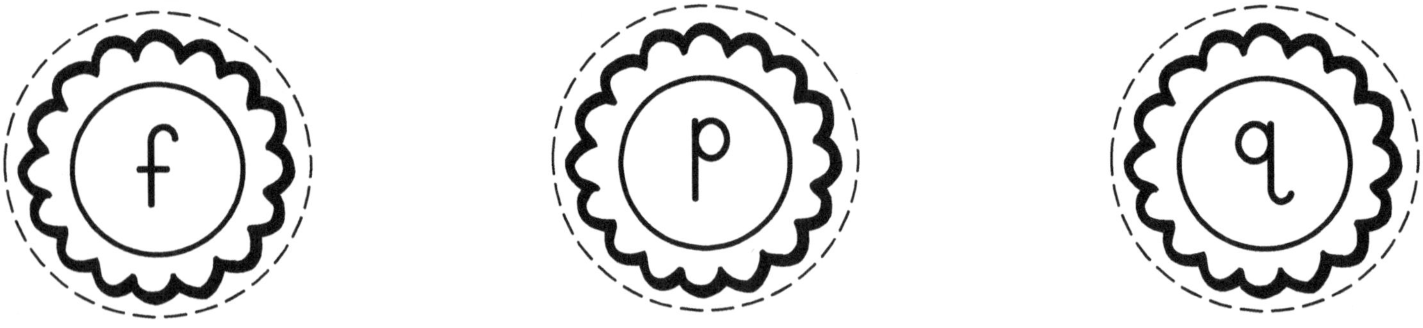

Squirrels and Nuts

Pocket Game

Matching Pictures to Ending Sound Letters A, F, G, K, L, M, N, R, S, T

Assembly

Reproduce, cut out, and glue a set of oak tag handles (p. 192) to a standard-size file folder. Option: Decorate each handle with a copy of the leaves on this page. Reproduce, color, and cut out the "Squirrels and Nuts" patterns. Matching in the center, glue the game board patterns to the inside of the folder. Apply glue only along the bottom and side edges, then attach each letter pail to a squirrel on the game board. Glue the cover art to the front of the folder. Decorate the border around the game board. Glue an envelope to the back of the folder for nut storage. Option: Reproduce, cut out, and glue the Pocket Game Playing Directions to the back of the folder. Note: Make additional "Squirrels and Nuts" pocket folders with different combinations of letter pails.

Squirrels and Nuts Cover
Matching Pictures to Ending Sound Letters A, F, G, K, L, M, N, R, S, T

Pocket Game

Squirrels and Nuts

Pocket Game

Matching Pictures to Ending Sound Letters A, F, G, K, L, M, N, R, S, T

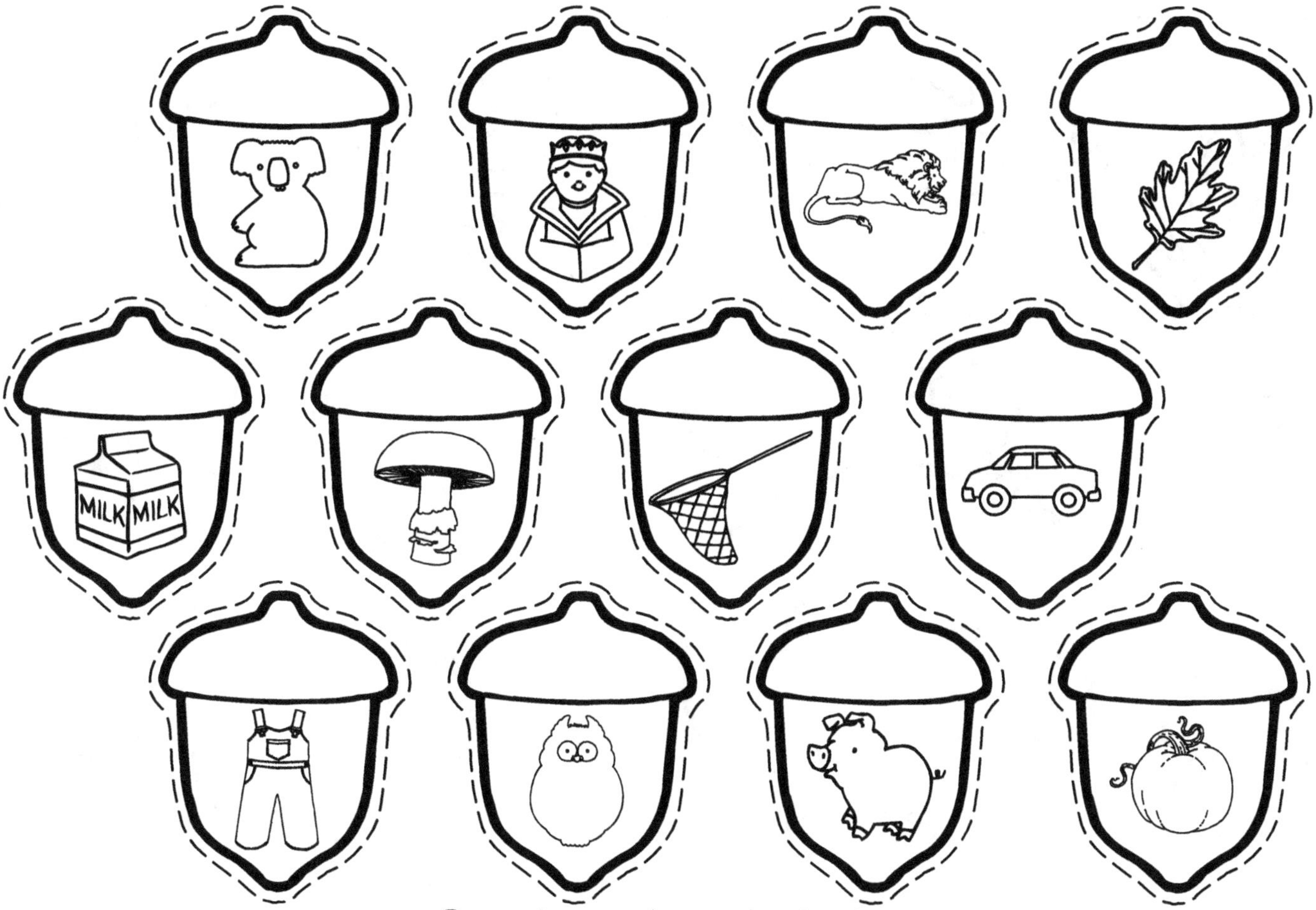

Reproduce, color, and cut out.
Apply glue only along the bottom and side edges of each letter pail.

a	g	n	f
k	m	t	r
s	l	g	n

Attach the pails to squirrels on the Squirrels and Nuts pocket boards.

Squirrels and Nuts

Matching Pictures to Ending Sound Letters A, F, G, K, L, M, N, R, S, T

Pocket Game

Squirrels and Nuts

Pocket Game

Matching Pictures to Ending Sound Letters A, F, G, K, L, M, N, R, S, T

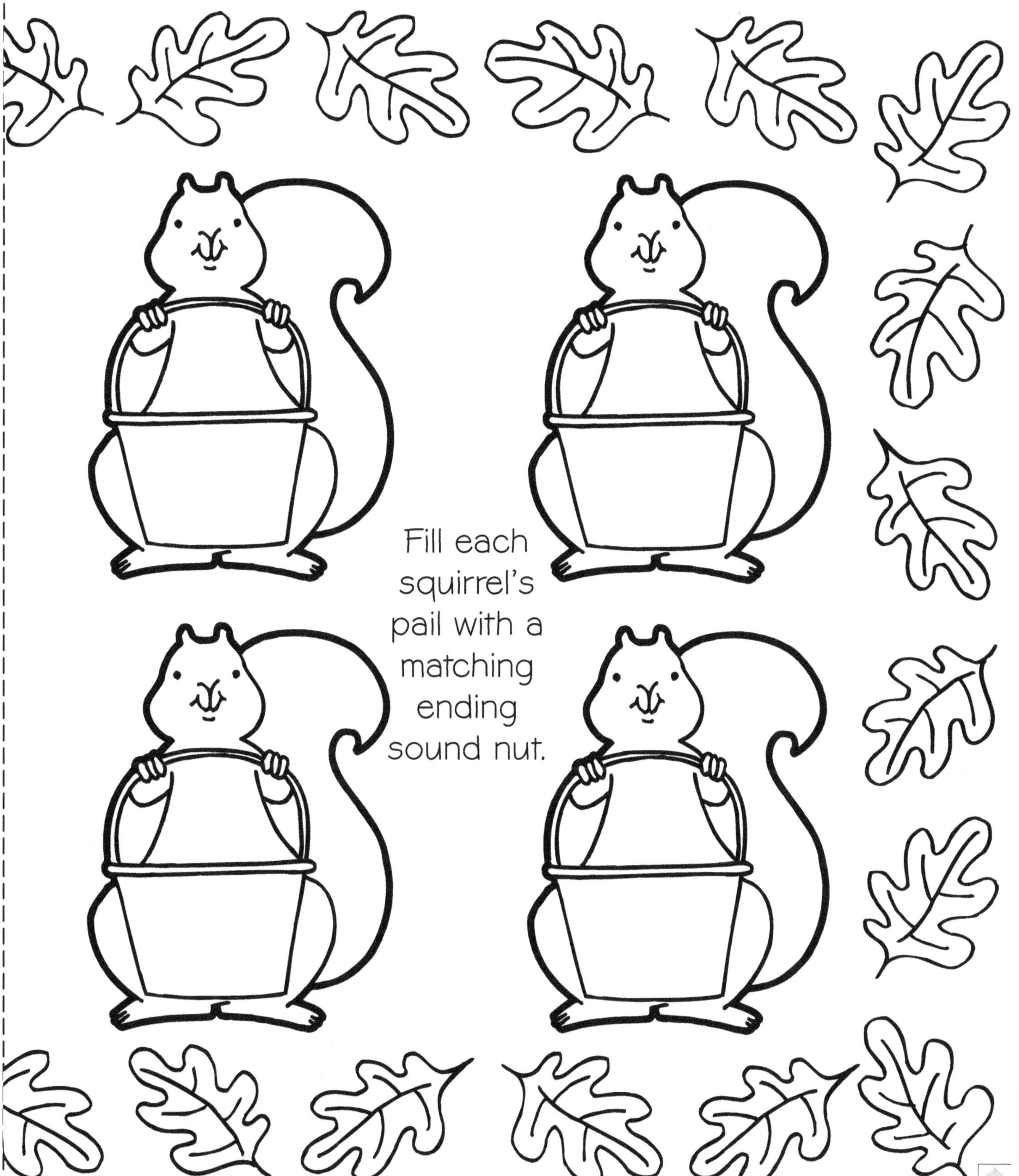

Fill each squirrel's pail with a matching ending sound nut.

Party Lanterns Lotto
Matching Pictures to Ending Sound Letters N, O, P, R, S

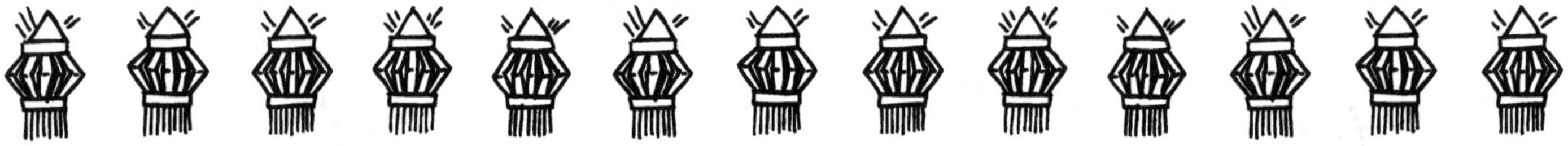

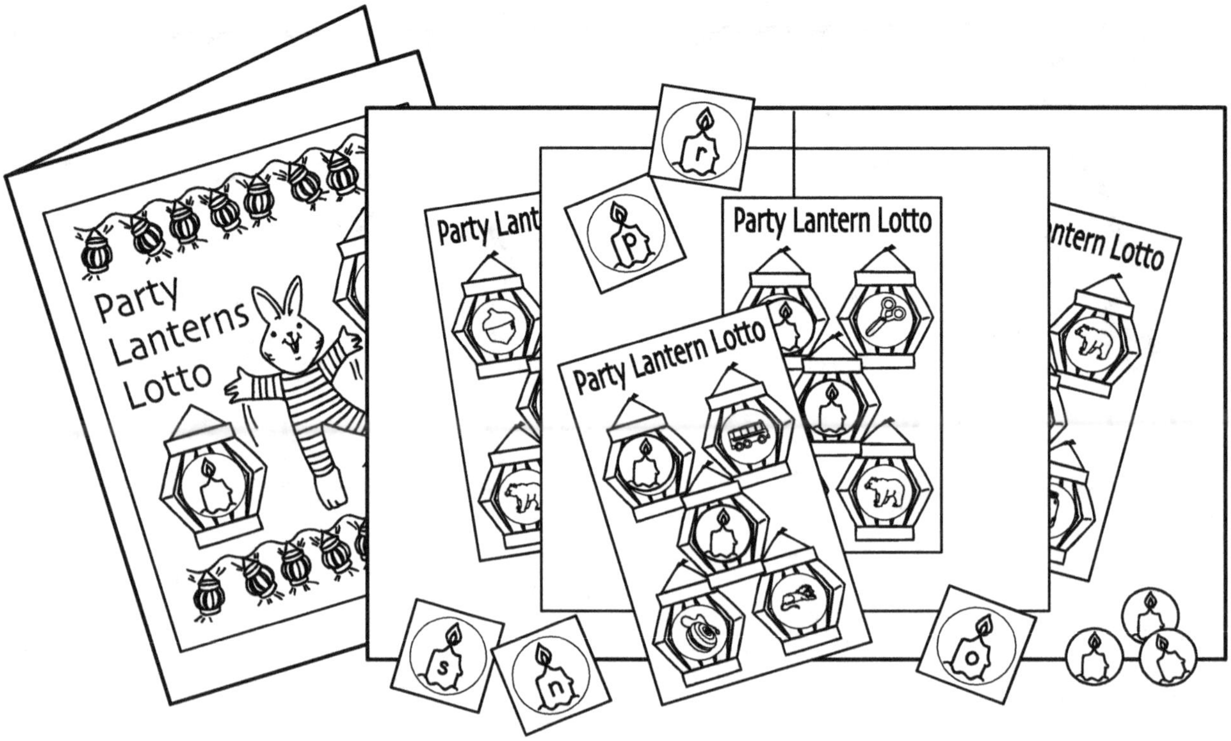

Lotto

Assembly

Reproduce, cut out, and glue a set of oak tag handles (p. 192) to a standard-size file folder. Option: Decorate each handle with copies of the lanterns shown above. Reproduce, color, and cut out the "Party Lanterns Lotto" patterns. Glue the cover art to the front of the folder. Mount Lotto boards on colored construction paper, then laminate. Glue two envelopes to the inside of the folder for Lotto board, token, and card storage. Option: Reproduce, cut out, and glue the Lotto Playing Directions to the back of the folder. Note: Wipe-off markers or crayons can also be used to color in matches.

Tokens
Reproduce, color, and cut out a set of tokens for each player.

Party Lanterns Lotto Cover
Matching Pictures to Ending Sound Letters N, O, P, R, S

Lotto

Party Lanterns Lotto

Party Lanterns Lotto
Matching Pictures to Ending Sound Letters N, O, P, R, S

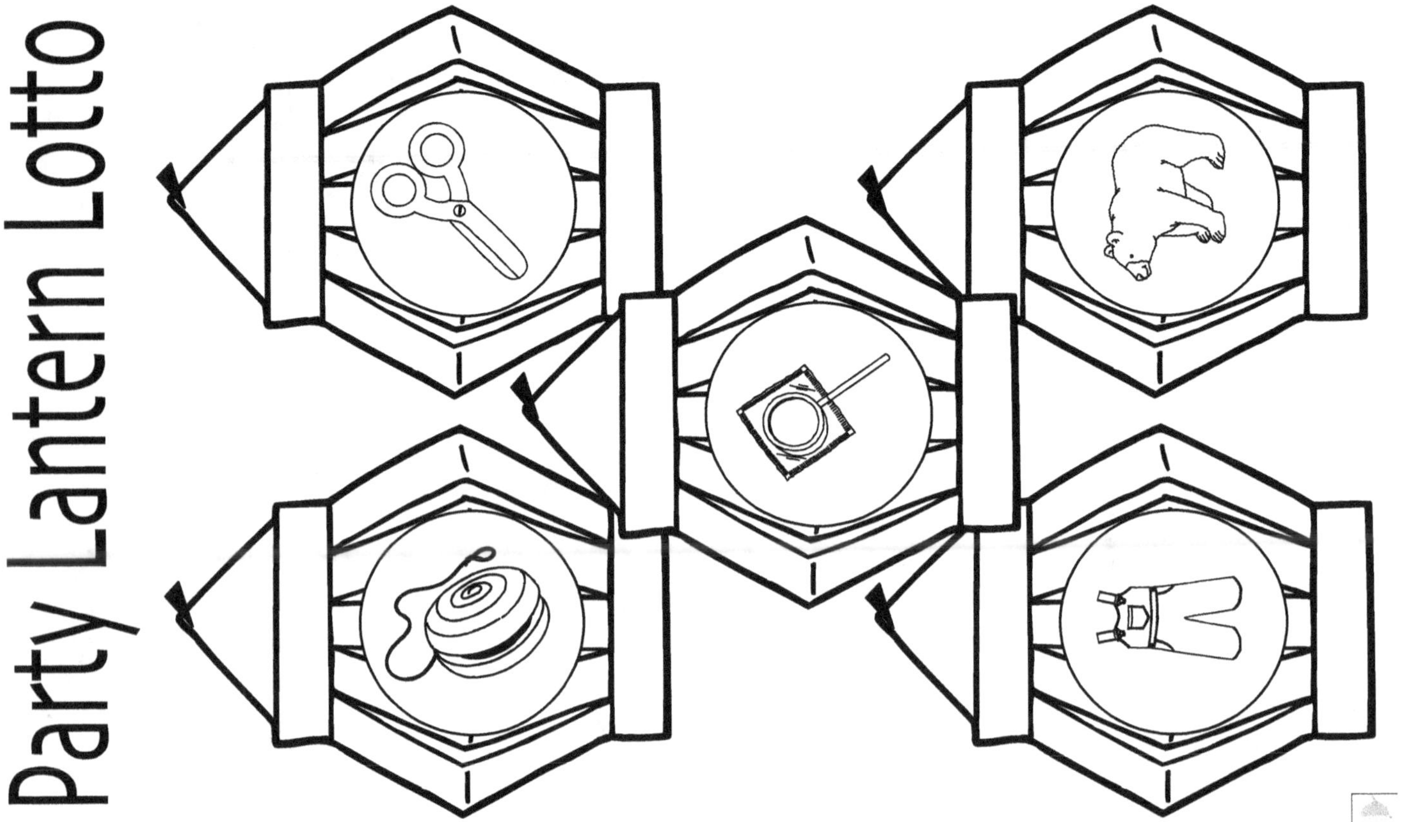

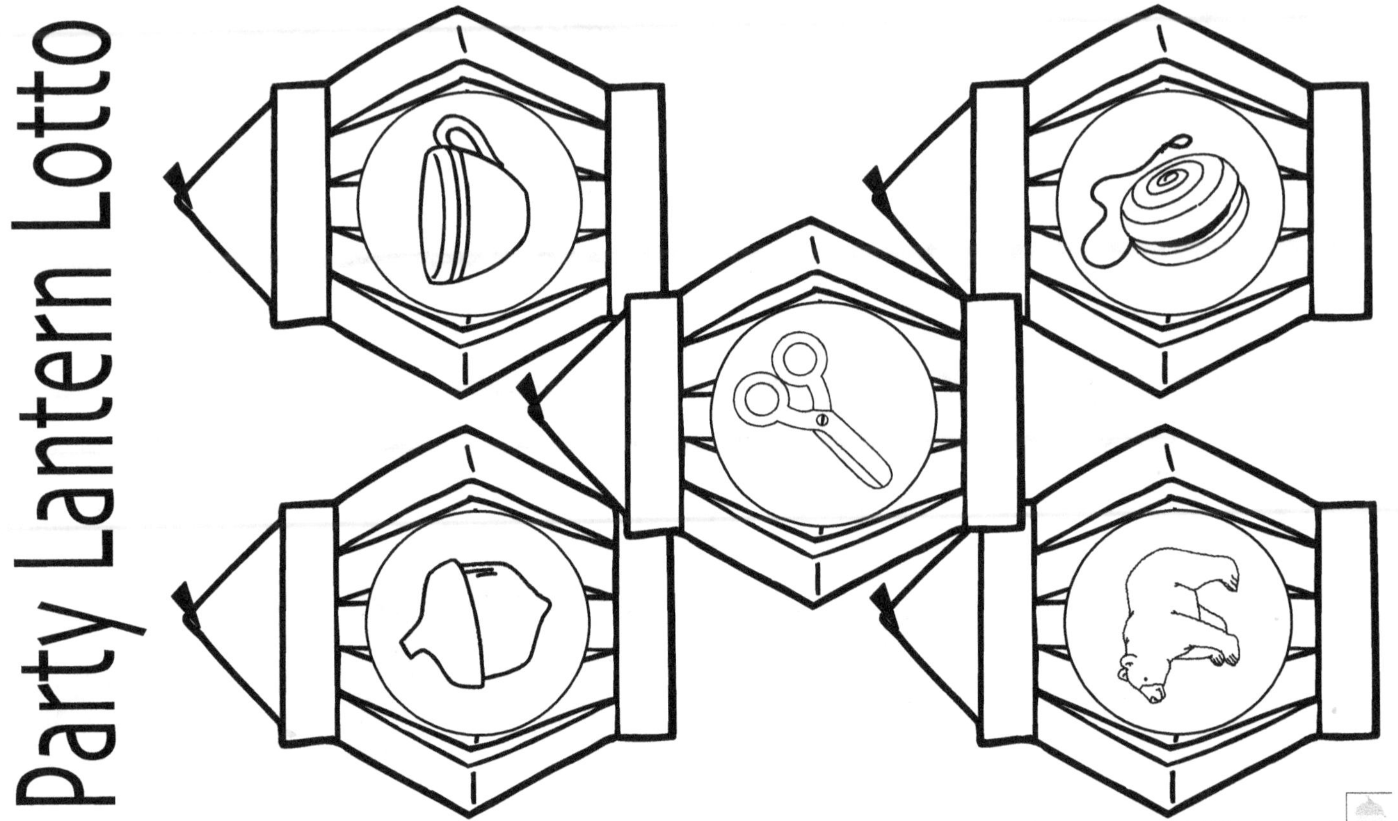

Lotto

Party Lanterns Lotto
Matching Pictures to Ending Sound Letters N, O, P, R, S

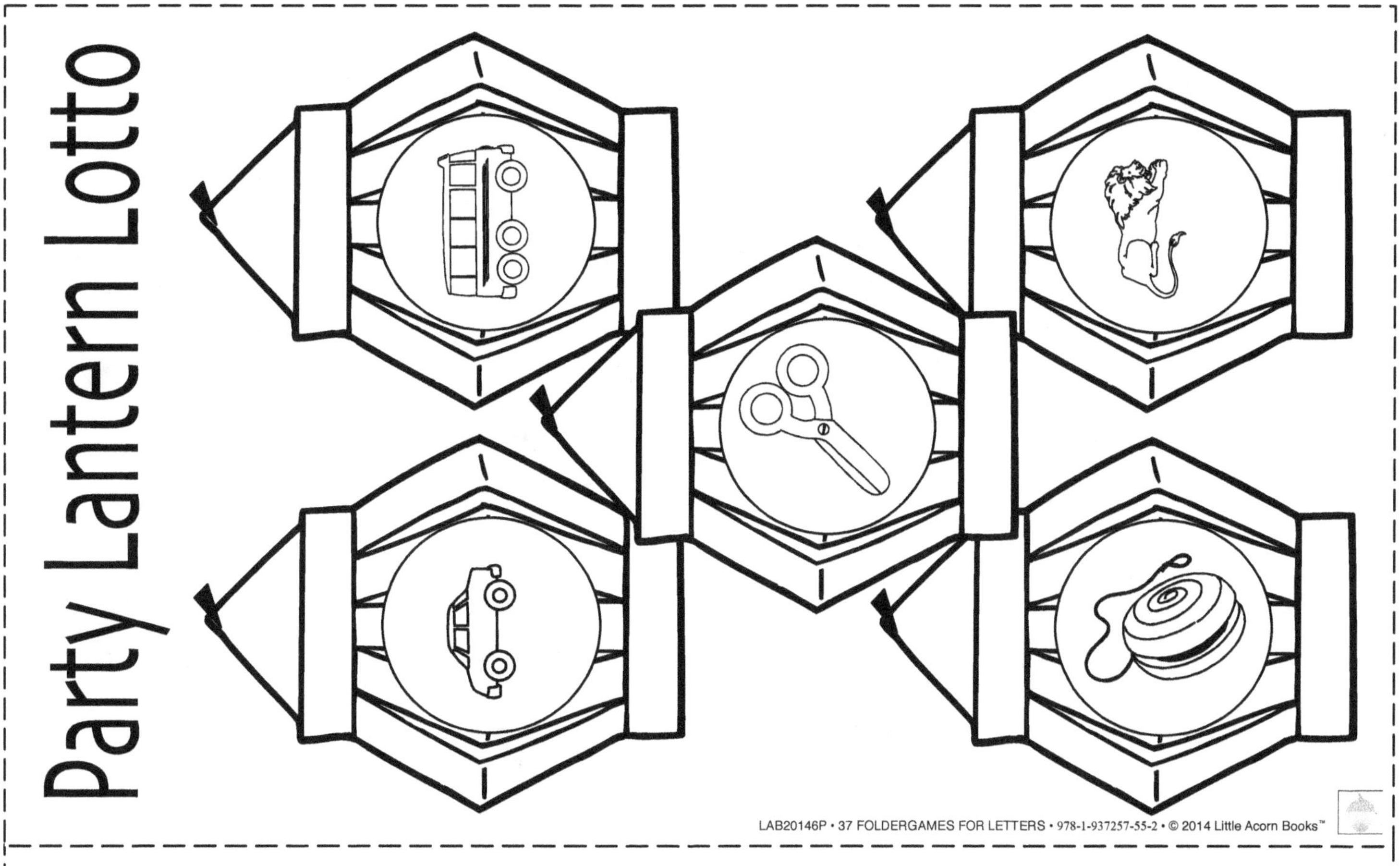

Party Lanterns Lotto
Matching Pictures to Ending Sound Letters N, O, P, R, S

Lotto

Reproduce, color, and cut out the cards.

Shells on the Shore

Fill-ins

Matching Pictures to Ending Sound Letters D, E, G, L, N, O, P, R, S, T, X

Assembly

Reproduce, cut out, and glue a set of oak tag handles (p. 192) to a standard-size file folder. Option: Decorate the handles with copies of the shells shown on this page. Reproduce, color, and cut out the "Shells on the Shore" patterns. Glue the fill-in boards to the inside of the folder. Glue the cover art to the front of the folder. Decorate the border around the fill-in boards, then laminate. Glue an envelope to the back of the folder for wipe-off marker or crayon storage. Option: Reproduce, cut out, and glue the Fill-ins Playing Directions to the back of the folder.

Shells on the Shore

Fill-ins

Matching Pictures to Ending Sound Letters D, E, G, L, N, O, P, R, S, T, X

Write the matching ending sound letter under each shell.

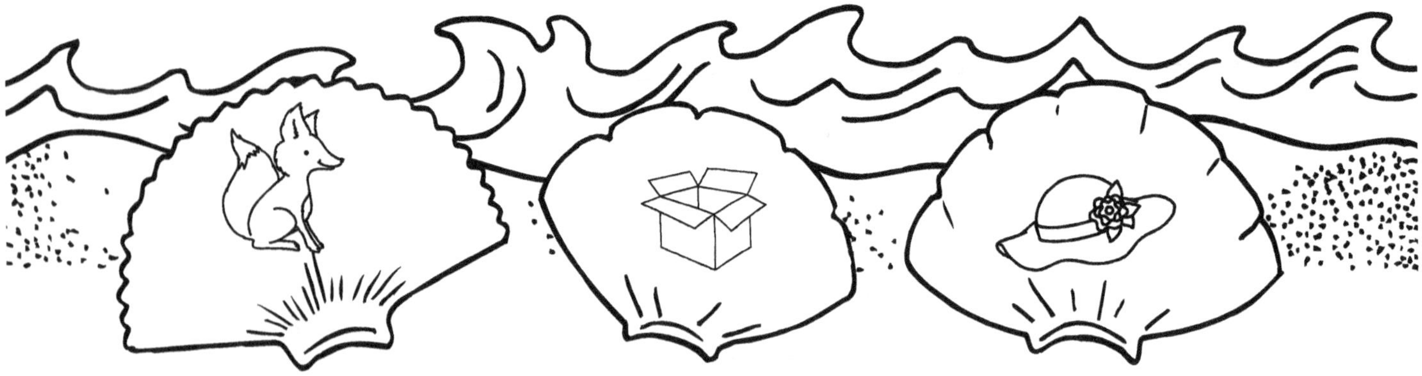

___   ___   ___

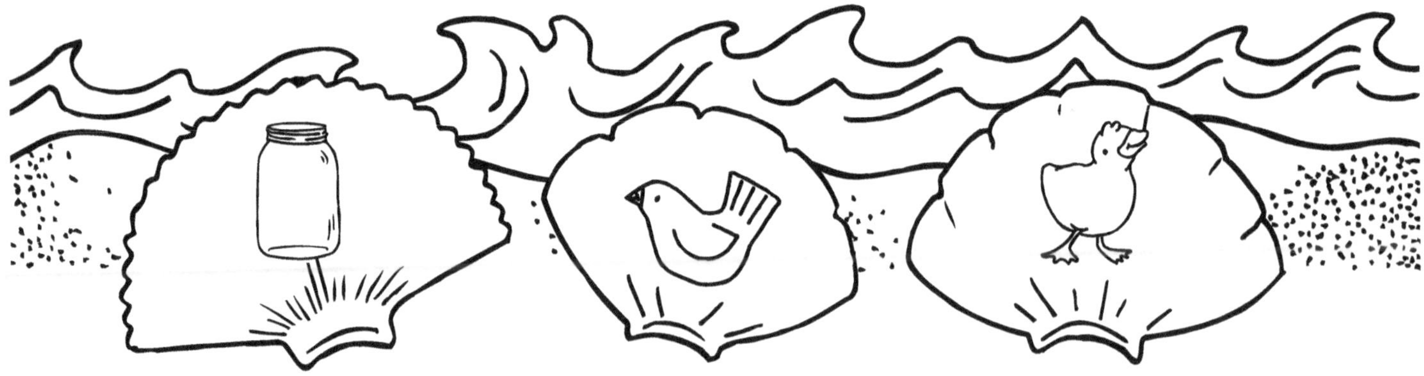

___   ___   ___

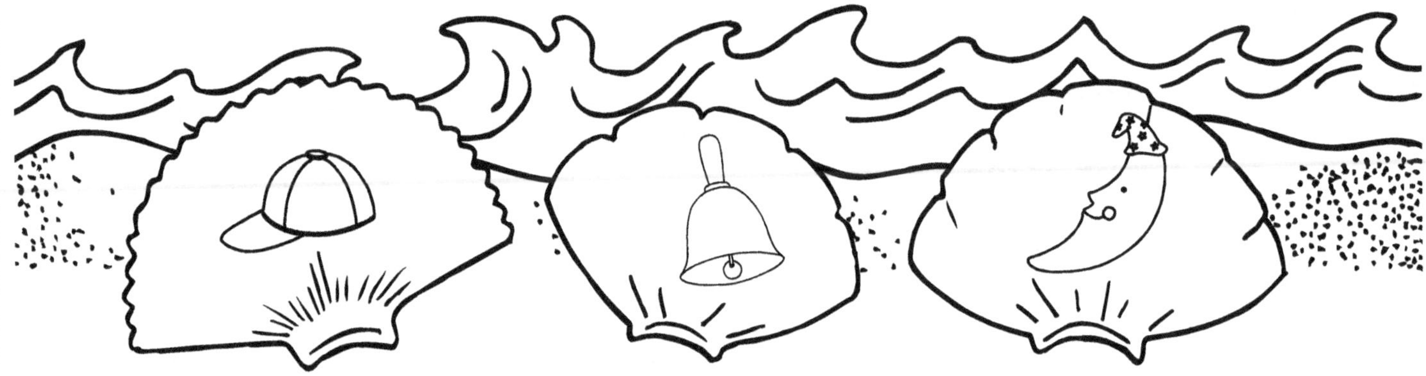

___   ___   ___

Shells on the Shore

Fill-ins

Matching Pictures to Ending Sound Letters D, E, G, L, N, O, P, R, S, T, X

Write the matching ending sound letter under each shell.

Shells on the Shore Cover

Matching Pictures to Ending Sound Letters D, E, G, L, N, O, P, R, S, T, X

Fill-ins

Stained Glass Butterfly

Color-by-Letter

Differentiating Letters B, b, D, d, A, a, G, g, S, s, U, u

Assembly

Reproduce, cut out, and glue a set of oak tag handles (p. 192) to a standard-size file folder. Option: Decorate each handle with a copy of the flowers on this page. Reproduce, color, and cut out the "Stained Glass Butterfly" patterns. Matching in the center, glue the game board patterns to the inside of the folder. Program the color code. Glue the cover art to the front of the folder. Decorate the border around the game board, then laminate. Glue an envelope to the back of the folder for wipe-off crayon or marker storage. Option: Reproduce, cut out, and glue the Color-by-Letter Playing Directions to the back of the folder. Reprogram the game board with letters O Q, U V, u v, and p q for additional letter skills practice.

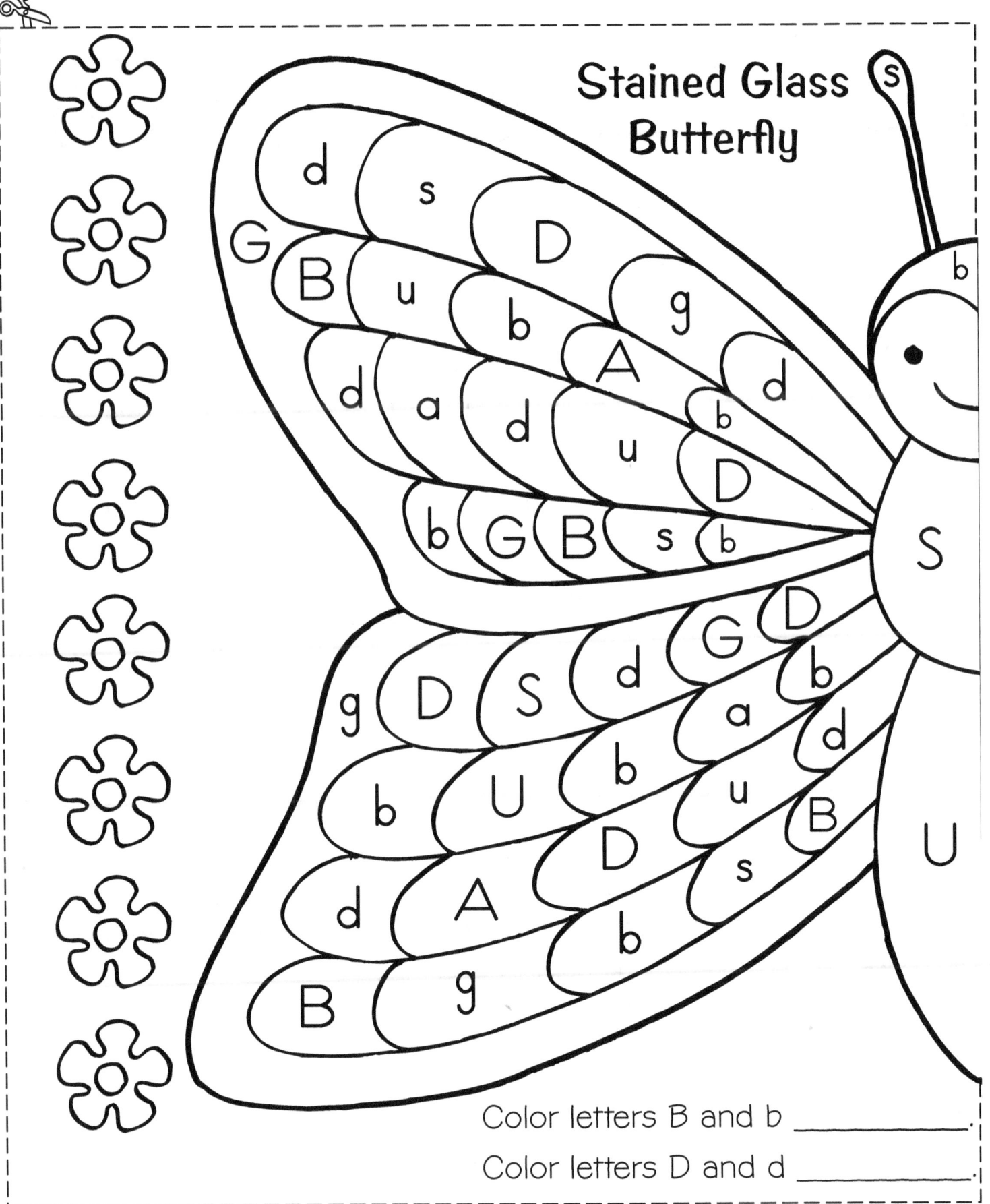

Stained Glass Butterfly Cover
Differentiating Letters B, b, D, d, A, a, G, g, S, s, U, u

Color-by-Letter

Stained Glass Butterfly

The Queen's Quilt
Differentiating Letters O, o, Q, q, p

Color-by-Letter

Assembly

Reproduce, cut out, and glue a set of oak tag handles (p. 192) to a standard-size file folder. Option: Decorate each handle with a copy of the crowns on this page. Reproduce, color, and cut out "The Queen's Quilt" patterns. Matching in the center, glue the game board patterns to the inside of the folder. Program the color code at the bottom of each board. Glue the cover art to the front of the folder. Decorate the border around the game board, then laminate. Glue an envelope to the back of the folder for wipe-off crayon or marker storage. Option: Reproduce, cut out, and glue the Color-by-Letter Playing Directions to the back of the folder. Reprogram the game board with letters B, b, D, d, and U, u, V, v for additional letter skills practice.

The Queen's Quilt

Differentiating Letters O, o, Q, q, p

Color-by-Letter

Color letter O _____. Color letter Q _____.
Color letter o _____.

The Queen's Quilt
Differentiating Letters O, o, Q, q, p

Color-by-Letter

Color letter q _____. Color letter p _____.

The Queen's Quilt Cover
Differentiating Letters O, o, Q, q, p

Color-by-Letter

The King's Kite
Differentiating Letters U, u, V, v, B, d, o

Color-by-Letter

Assembly

Reproduce, cut out, and glue a set of oak tag handles (p. 192) to a standard-size file folder. Option: Decorate each handle with a copy of the kites on this page. Reproduce, color, and cut out "The King's Kite" patterns. Matching in the center, glue the game board patterns to the inside of the folder. Program the code on the board. Glue the cover art to the front of the folder. Decorate the border around the game board, then laminate. Glue an envelope to the back of the folder for wipe-off crayon or marker storage. Option: Reproduce, cut out, and glue the Color-by-Letter Playing Directions to the back of the folder. Reprogram the game board with letters O, o, Q, q, and B, b, D, d for additional letter skills practice.

The King's Kite

Differentiating Letters U, u, V, v, b, d, o

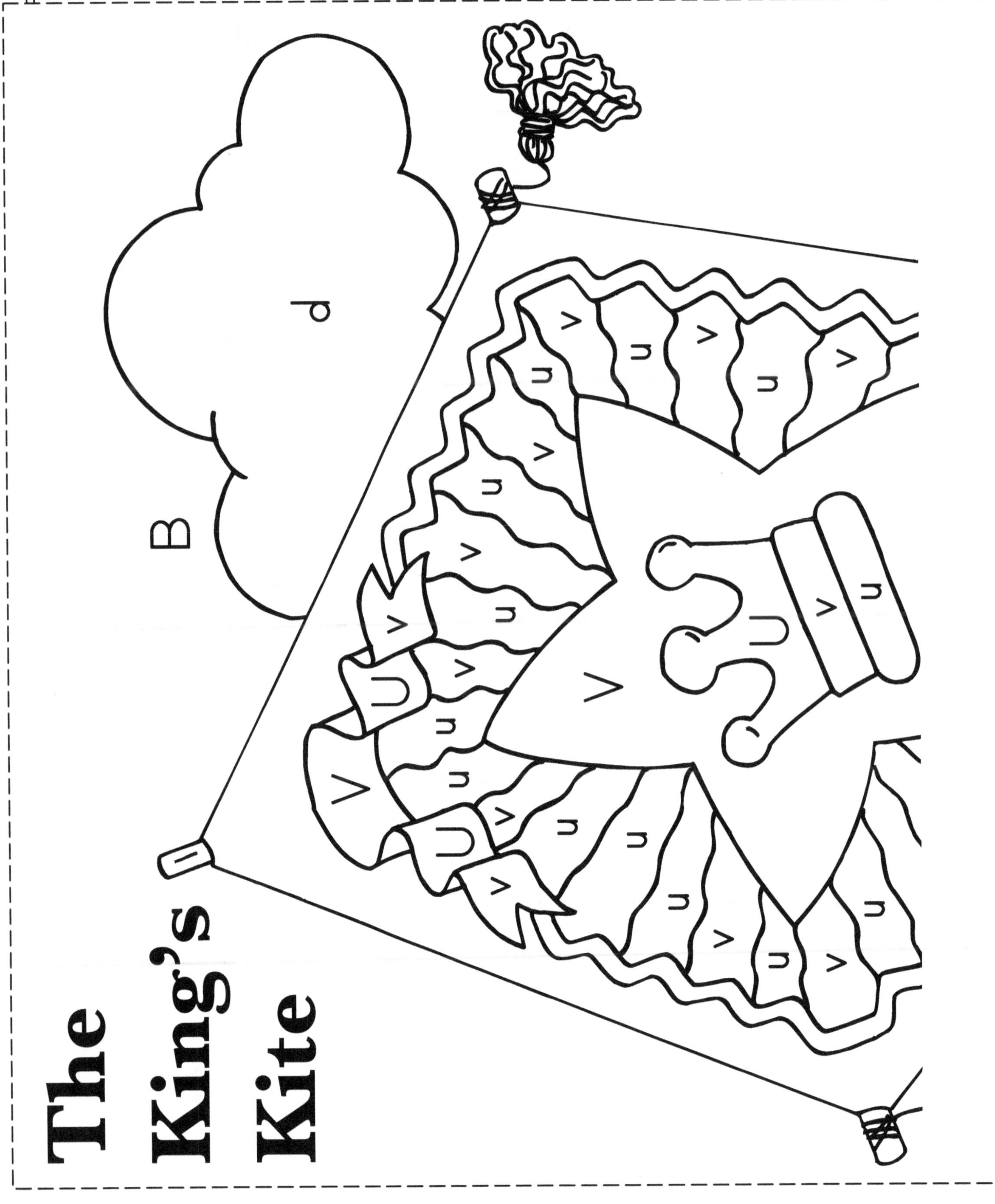

Color-by-Letter

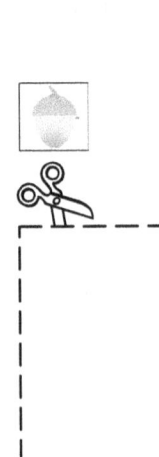

146 LAB20146P • 37 FOLDERGAMES FOR LETTERS • 978-1-937257-55-2 • © 2014 Little Acorn Books™

The King's Kite

Differentiating Letters U, u, V, v, b, d, o

Color-by-Letter

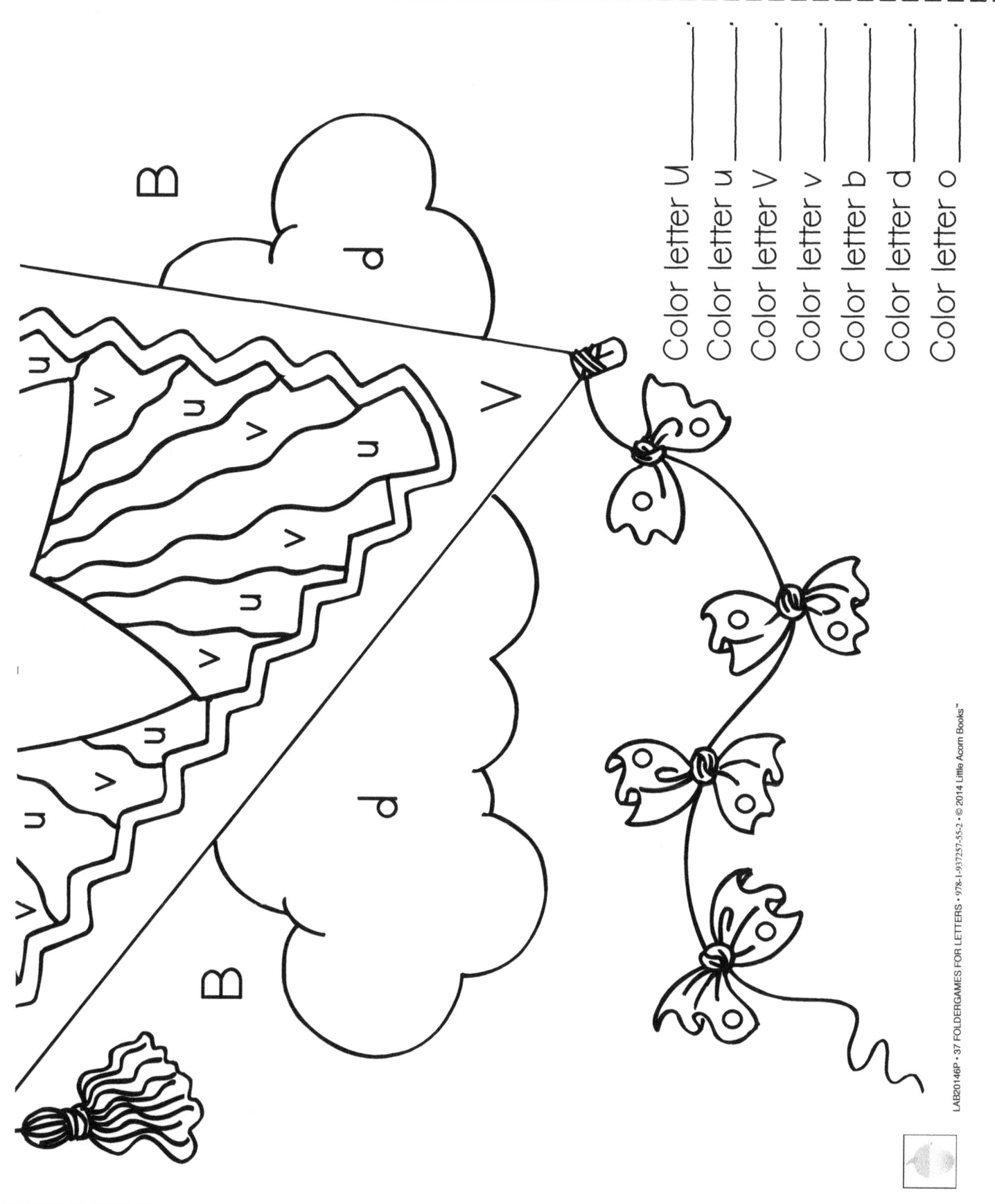

Color letter U
Color letter u
Color letter V
Color letter v
Color letter b
Color letter d
Color letter o

The King's Kite Cover
Differentiating Letters U, u, V, v, B, d, o

Color-by-Letter

Bumble Bee Boogie
Matching Uppercase and Lowercase Consonants

Clothespin Match-up

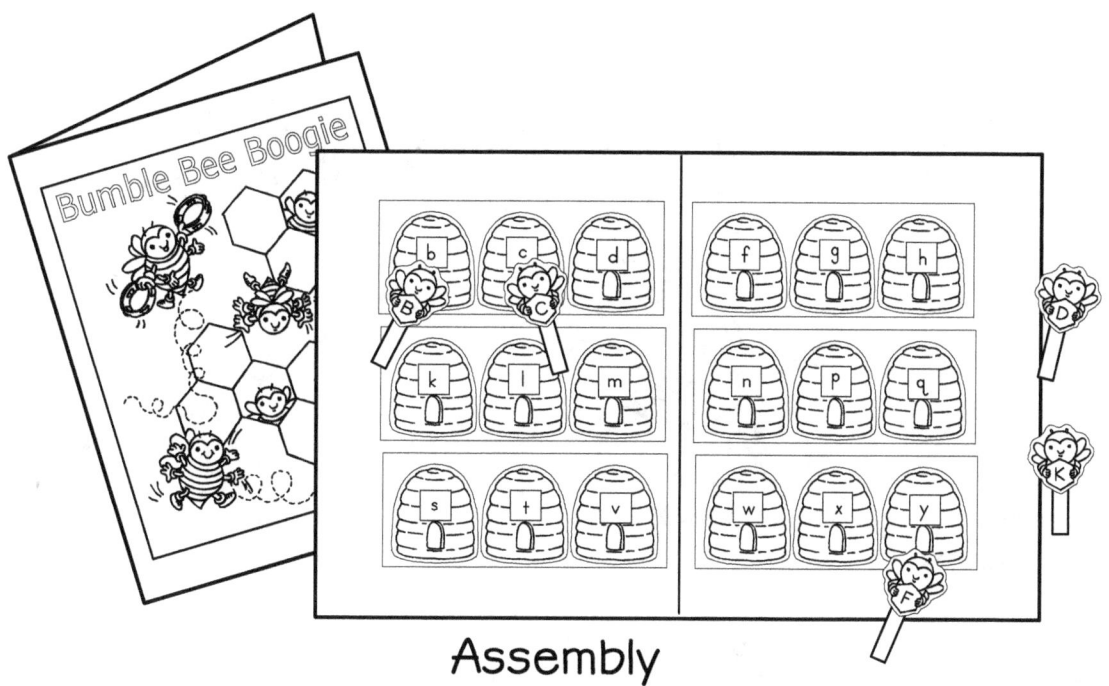

Assembly
Reproduce, cut out, and glue a set of oak tag handles (p. 192) to a standard-size file folder. Option: Color black and yellow stripes on the handles. Reproduce, color, and cut out the "Bumble Bee Boogie" patterns. Glue the uppercase consonant bees on clothespins. Glue a lowercase consonant card on each beehive, then glue the hives on the beehive strips. Glue the assembled beehive strips to the inside of the folder. Glue the cover art to the front of the folder. Decorate the border around the game board. Staple a resealable plastic bag to the back of the folder for clothespin storage. Options: Reproduce, cut out, and glue the Clothespin Match-ups directions to the back of the folder. Make additional game boards programmed with the remaining consonant cards and bees.

Lowercase Consonant Cards
Reproduce, cut apart, and glue a card on each beehive.

b	c	d	f	g	h	j
k	l	m	n	p	q	r
s	t	v	w	x	y	z

Bumble Bee Boogie Cover — Clothespin Match-up
Matching Uppercase and Lowercase Consonants

Bumble Bee Boogie

Bumble Bee Boogie

Clothespin Match-up

Matching Uppercase and Lowercase Consonants

Reproduce, color, cut out, and glue six beehive strips to the inside of a folder.

Bumble Bee Boogie

Matching Uppercase and Lowercase Consonants

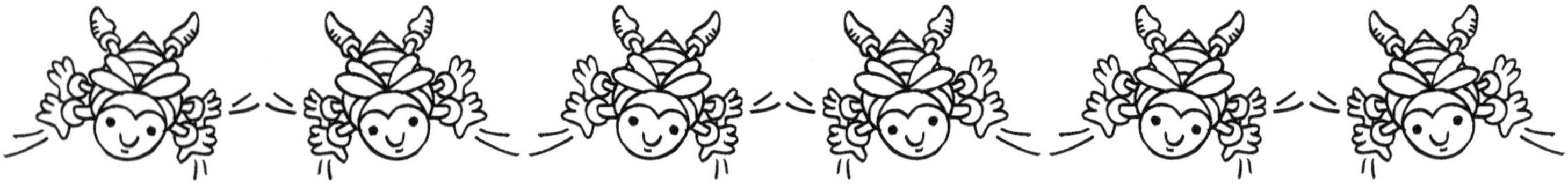

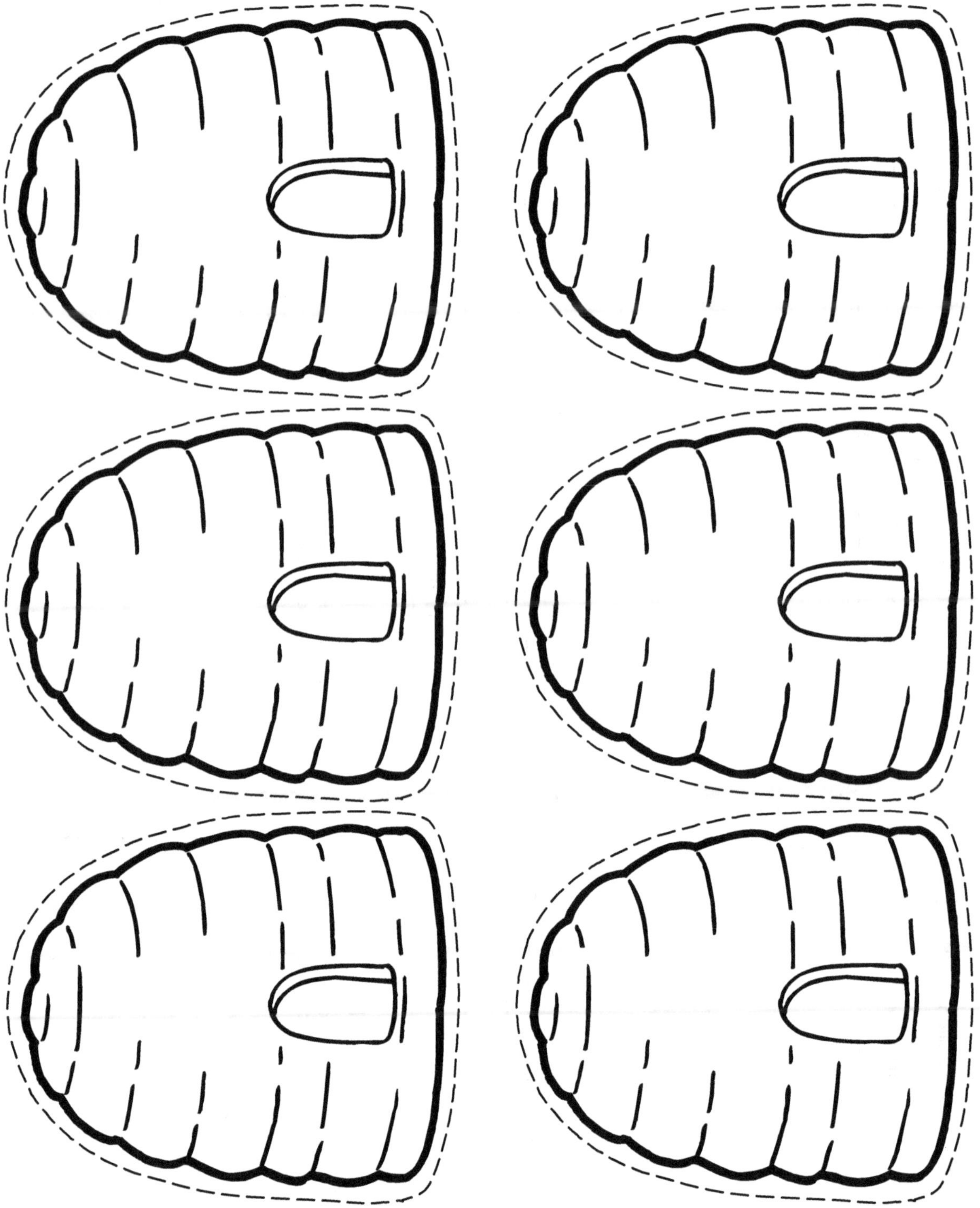

Clothespin Match-up

Reproduce three sets of beehives. Then glue a lowercase letter card on each beehive.
Do not glue down the bottom portion of hives.

Bumble Bee Boogie
Matching Uppercase and Lowercase Consonants

Clothespin Match-up

B C D F
G H J K
L M N P
Q R S T
V W Z X Y

Reproduce, color, cut out, and glue each bee on a clothespin.

Clownfish Carnival

Fill-ins

Matching Uppercase and Lowercase Consonants F, G, H, J, K

Assembly

Reproduce, cut out, and glue a set of oak tag handles (p. 192) to a standard-size file folder. Option: Draw blue waves or decorate the handles with copies of the fish shown on this page. Reproduce, color, and cut out the "Clownfish Carnival" patterns. Glue the fill-in boards to the inside of the folder. Glue the cover art to the front of the folder. Decorate the border around the fill-in boards, then laminate. Glue an envelope to the back of the folder for wipe-off marker or crayon storage. Option: Reproduce, cut out, and glue the Fill-ins Playing Directions to the back of the folder.

Clownfish Carnival Cover
Matching Uppercase and Lowercase Consonants F, G, H, J, K

Fill-ins

Clownfish Carnival

Fill-ins

Matching Uppercase and Lowercase Consonants F, G, H, J, K

Write the matching uppercase or lowercase letter on each fish.

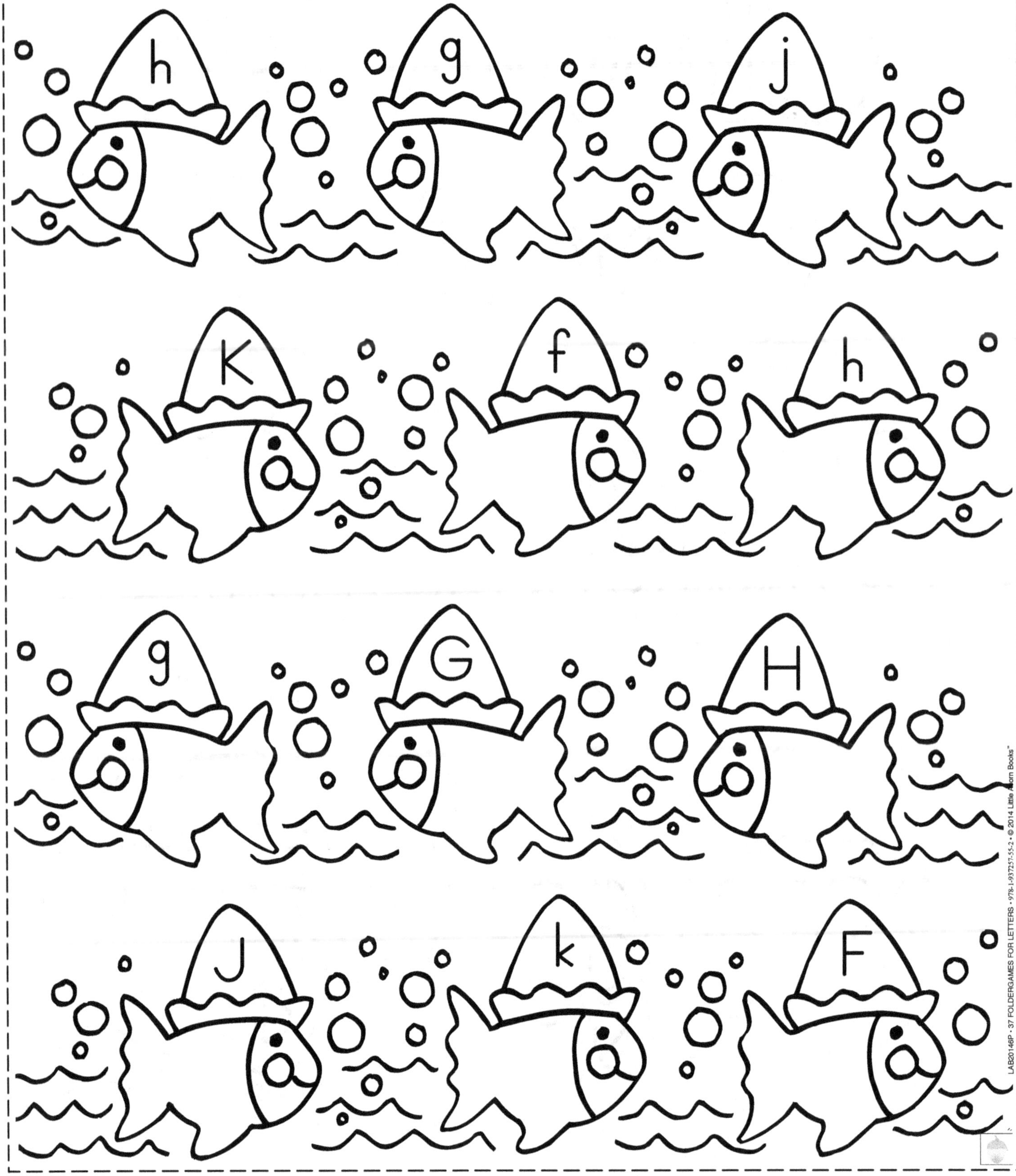

h	g	j
K	f	h
g	G	H
J	k	F

Clownfish Carnival
Matching Uppercase and Lowercase Consonants F, G, H, J, K

Fill-ins

Write the matching uppercase or lowercase letter on each fish.

Pigs in Blankets Lotto

Lotto

Matching Uppercase and Lowercase Consonants K, L, M, N, P

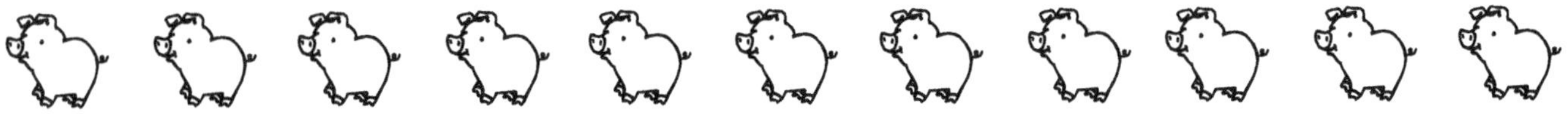

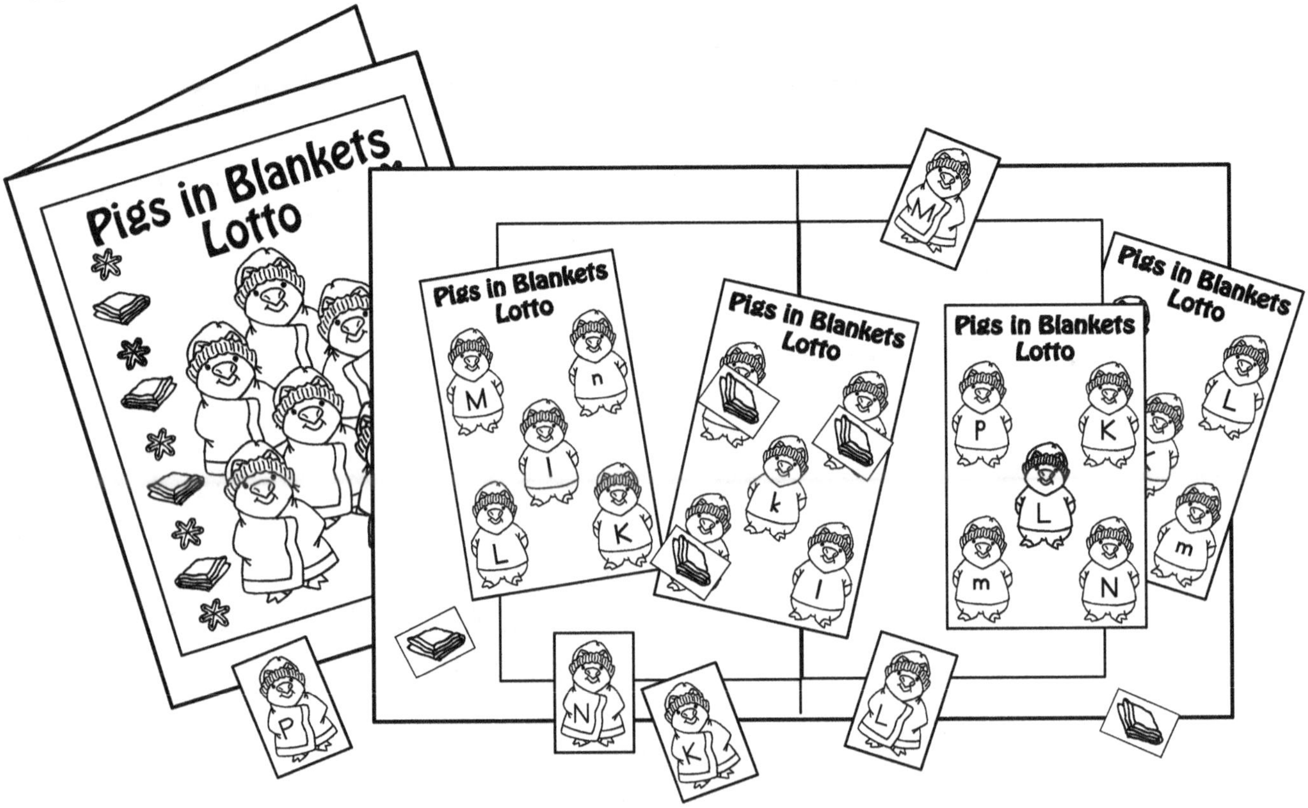

Assembly

Reproduce, cut out, and glue a set of oak tag handles (p. 192) to a standard-size file folder. Option: Decorate each handle with copies of the pigs shown above. Reproduce, color, and cut out the "Pigs in Blankets Lotto" patterns. Glue the cover art to the front of the folder. Mount Lotto boards on colored construction paper, then laminate. Glue two envelopes to the inside of the folder for Lotto board, token, and card storage. Option: Reproduce, cut out, and glue the Lotto Playing Directions to the back of the folder. Note: Wipe-off markers or crayons can also be used to color in matches.

Tokens

Reproduce, color, and cut out a set of tokens for each player.

Pigs in Blankets Lotto Cover
Matching Uppercase and Lowercase Consonants K, L, M, N, P

Lotto

Pigs in Blankets Lotto

Pigs in Blankets Lotto
Matching Uppercase and Lowercase Consonants K, L, M, N, P

Pigs in Blankets Lotto
Matching Uppercase and Lowercase Consonants K, L, M, N, P

Lotto

Pigs in Blankets Lotto
Matching Uppercase and Lowercase Consonants K, L, M, N, P

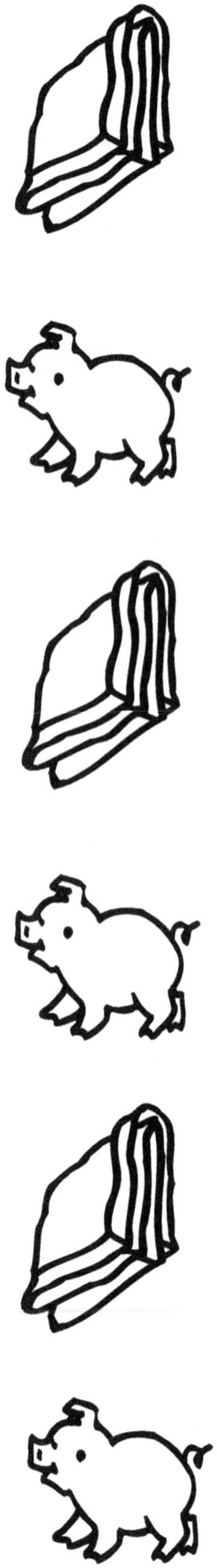

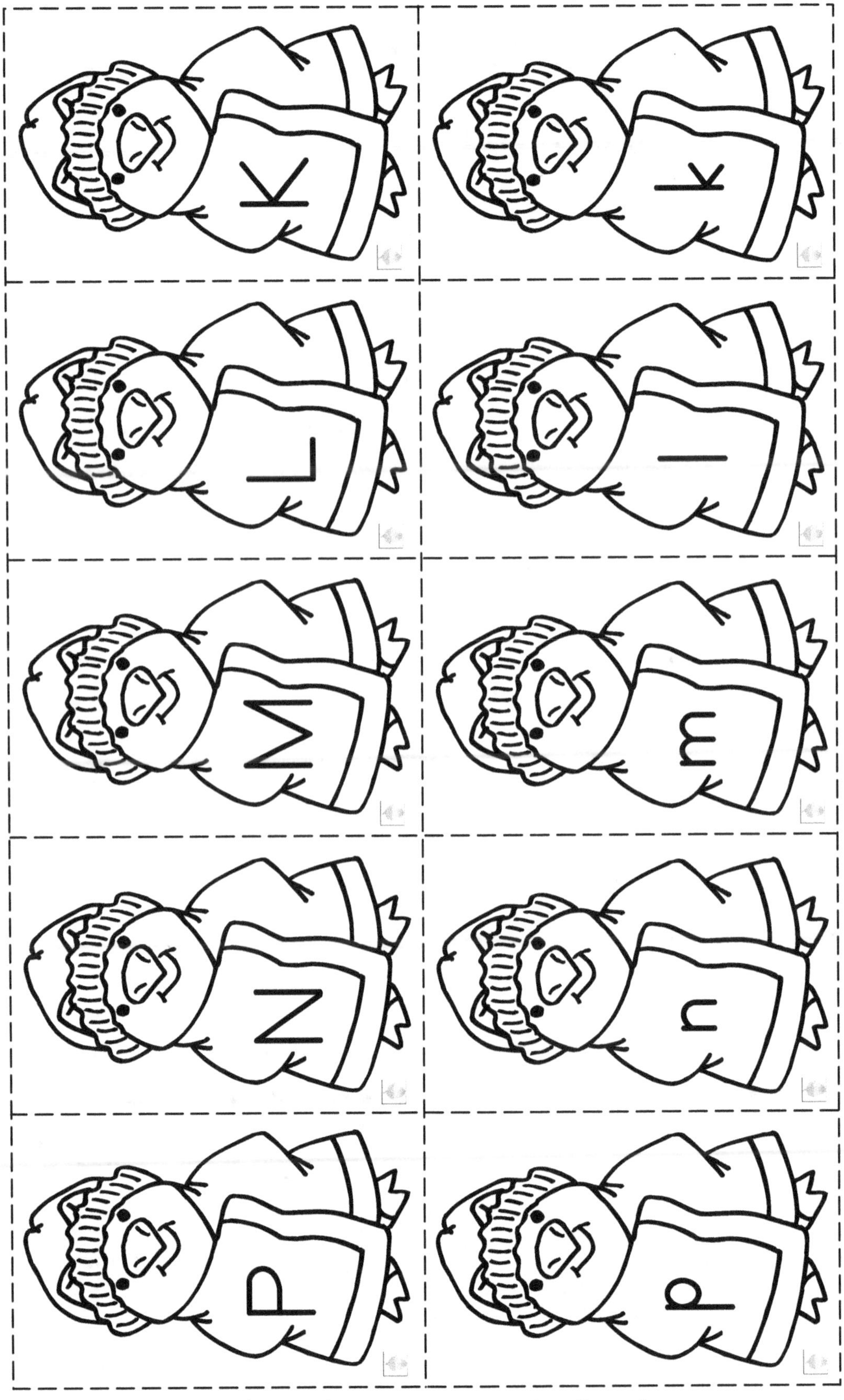

Lotto

Reproduce, color, and cut apart two sets of cards.

Funny Car Rally

Matching Uppercase and Lowercase Consonants P, Q, R, S, T

Trail Game

Assembly

Reproduce, cut out, and glue a set of oak tag handles (p. 192) to a standard-size file folder. Option: Decorate each handle with copies of the tires shown above. Reproduce, color, and cut out the "Funny Car Rally" patterns. Matching in the center, glue the game board patterns to the inside of the folder. Glue the cover art to the front of the folder. Decorate the border around the game board, then laminate. Reproduce, color, laminate, then cut out the pawns and two sets of tire game cards. Glue an envelope to the back of the folder for pawn and game card storage. Option: Reproduce, cut out, and glue the Trail Game Playing Directions to the back of the folder.

Pawns

Funny Car Rally

Funny Car Rally Cover
Matching Uppercase and Lowercase Consonants P, Q, R, S, T

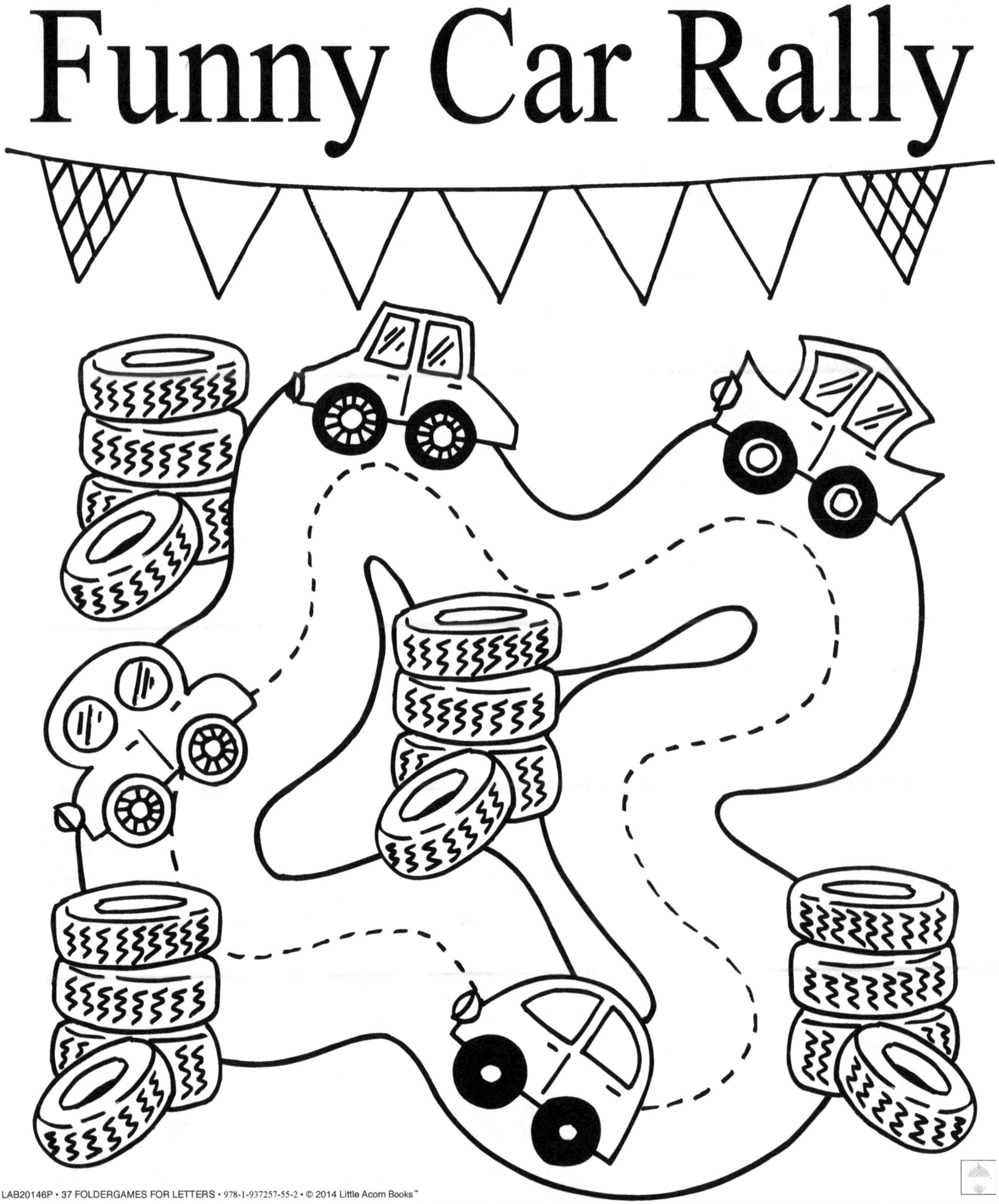

Trail Game

Funny Car Rally

Matching Uppercase and Lowercase Consonants P, Q, R, S, T

Trail Game

Reproduce, color, and cut apart two sets of cards.

Funny Car Rally

Matching Uppercase and Lowercase Consonants P, Q, R, S, T

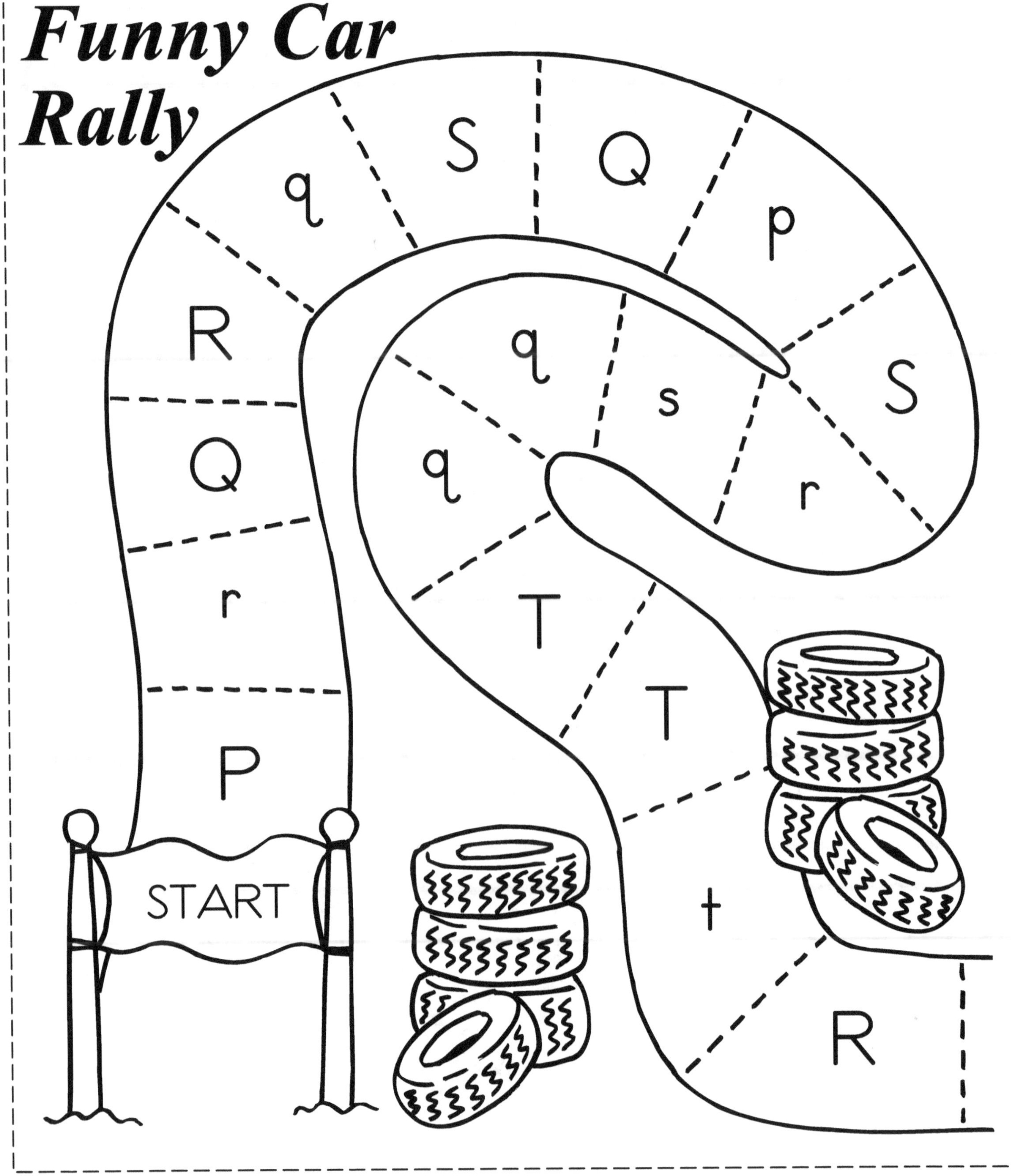

Trail Game

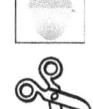

Funny Car Rally

Trail Game

Matching Uppercase and Lowercase Consonants P, Q, R, S, T

Help the cars get to the end of the race course.

Q r R S p t q T S t r P R P s T p

THE END

q Q P S t
R s P r T

Peek-a-boo Pumpkins

Pocket Game

Matching Uppercase and Lowercase Consonants V, W, X, Y, Z

Assembly

Reproduce, cut out, and glue a set of oak tag handles (p. 192) to a standard-size file folder. Option: Decorate each handle with a copy of the pumpkins on this page. Reproduce, color, and cut out the "Peek-a-boo Pumpkins" patterns. Glue two placement templates to the inside of the folder. Apply glue only along the bottom and side edges, then attach four bags to each template. Glue the cover art to the front of the folder. Decorate the border around the game board. Glue an envelope to the back of the folder for pumpkin storage. Option: Reproduce, cut out, and glue the Pocket Game Playing Directions to the back of the folder. Note: Make additional "Peek-a-boo Pumpkins" pocket folders with different combinations of bags.

Peek-a-boo Pumpkins Cover
Matching Uppercase and Lowercase Consonants V, W, X, Y, Z

Pocket Game

Peek-a-boo Pumpkins

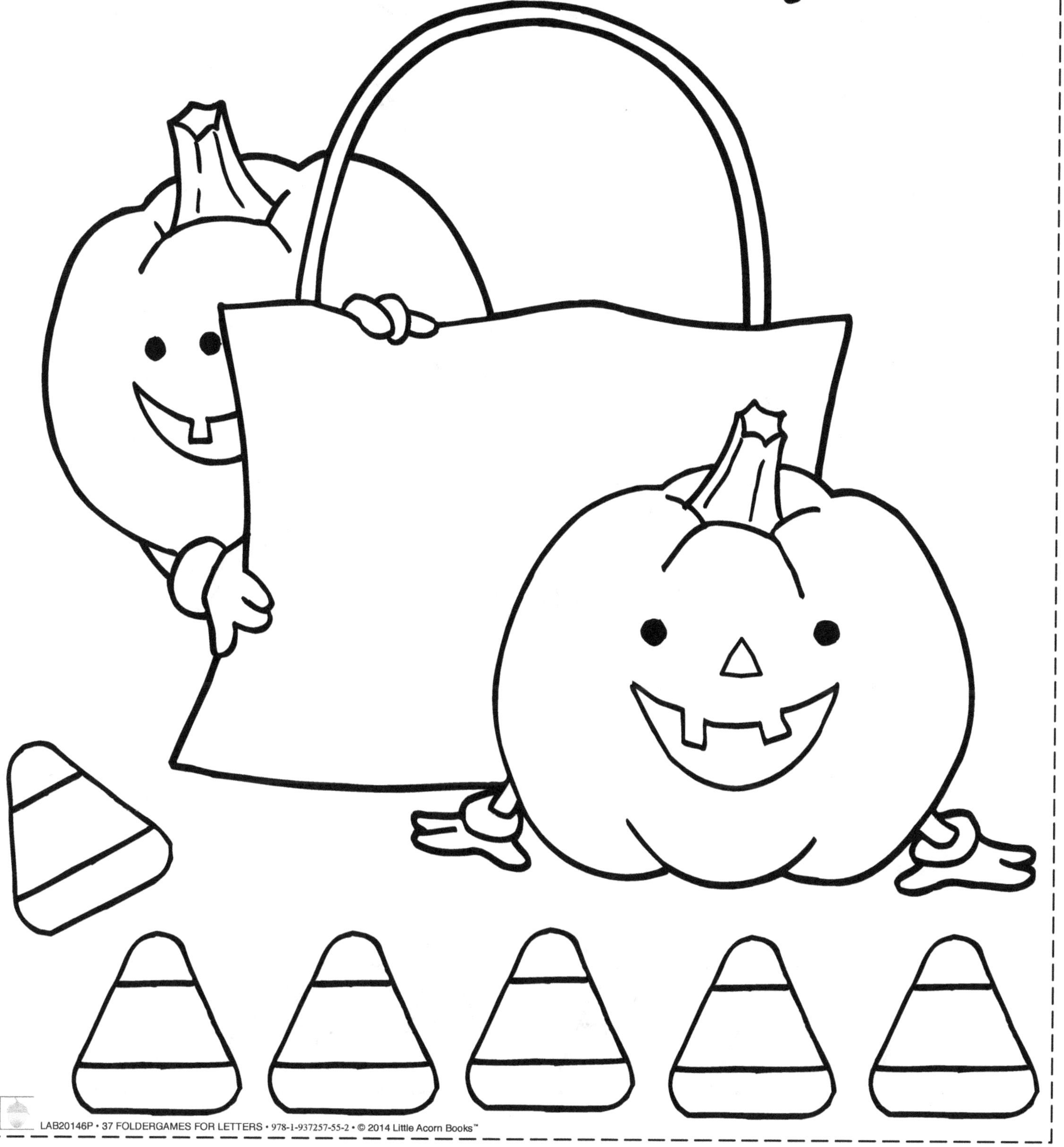

Peek-a-boo Pumpkins

Matching Uppercase and Lowercase Consonants V, W, X, Y, Z

Pocket Game

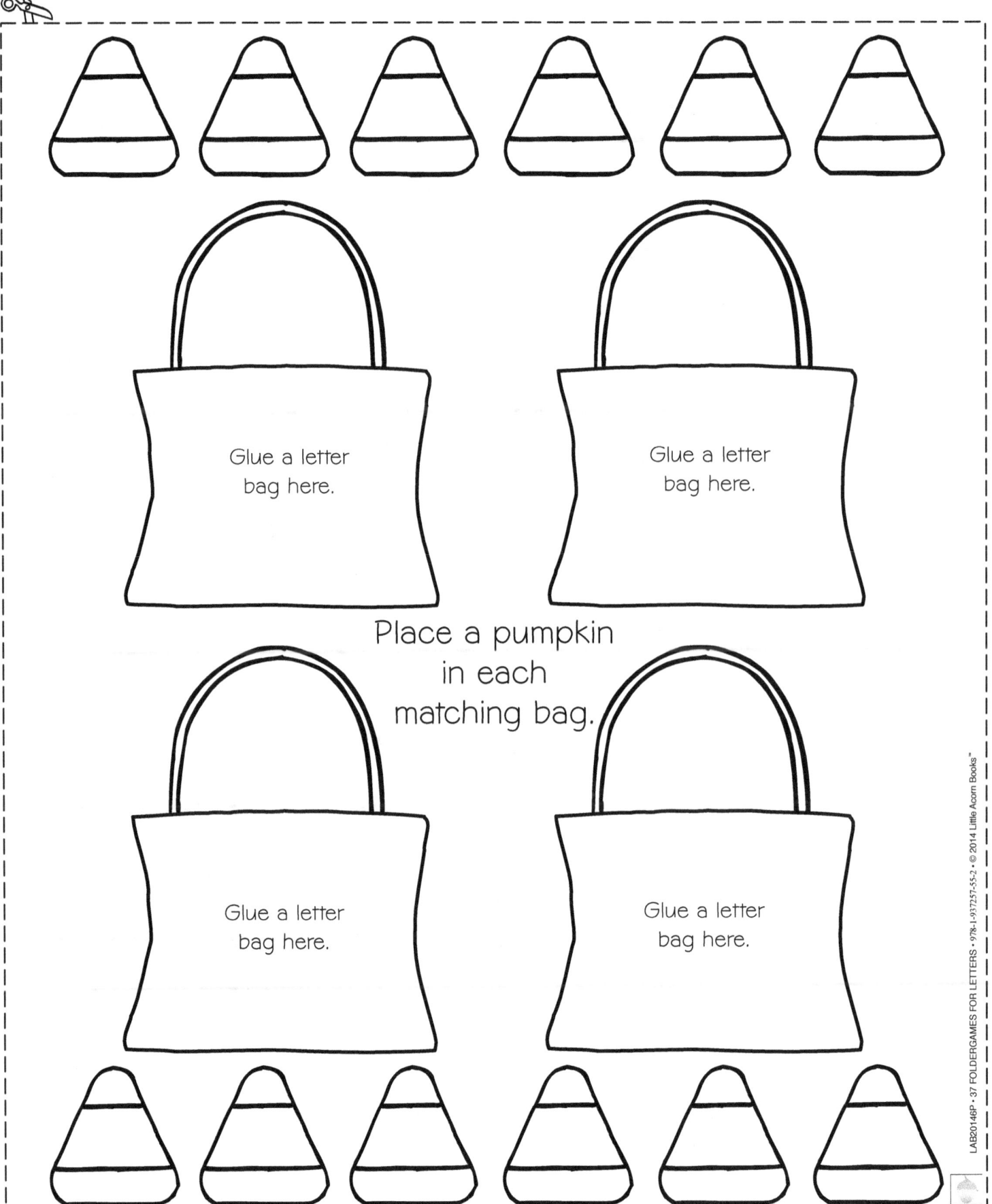

Peek-a-boo Pumpkins
Matching Uppercase and Lowercase Consonants V, W, X, Y, Z

Pocket Game

Reproduce, color, and cut out the bags. Apply glue only along the bottom and side edges of each bag. Then attach each bag to a placement template.

Peek-a-boo Pumpkins

Pocket Game

Matching Uppercase and Lowercase Consonants V, W, X, Y, Z

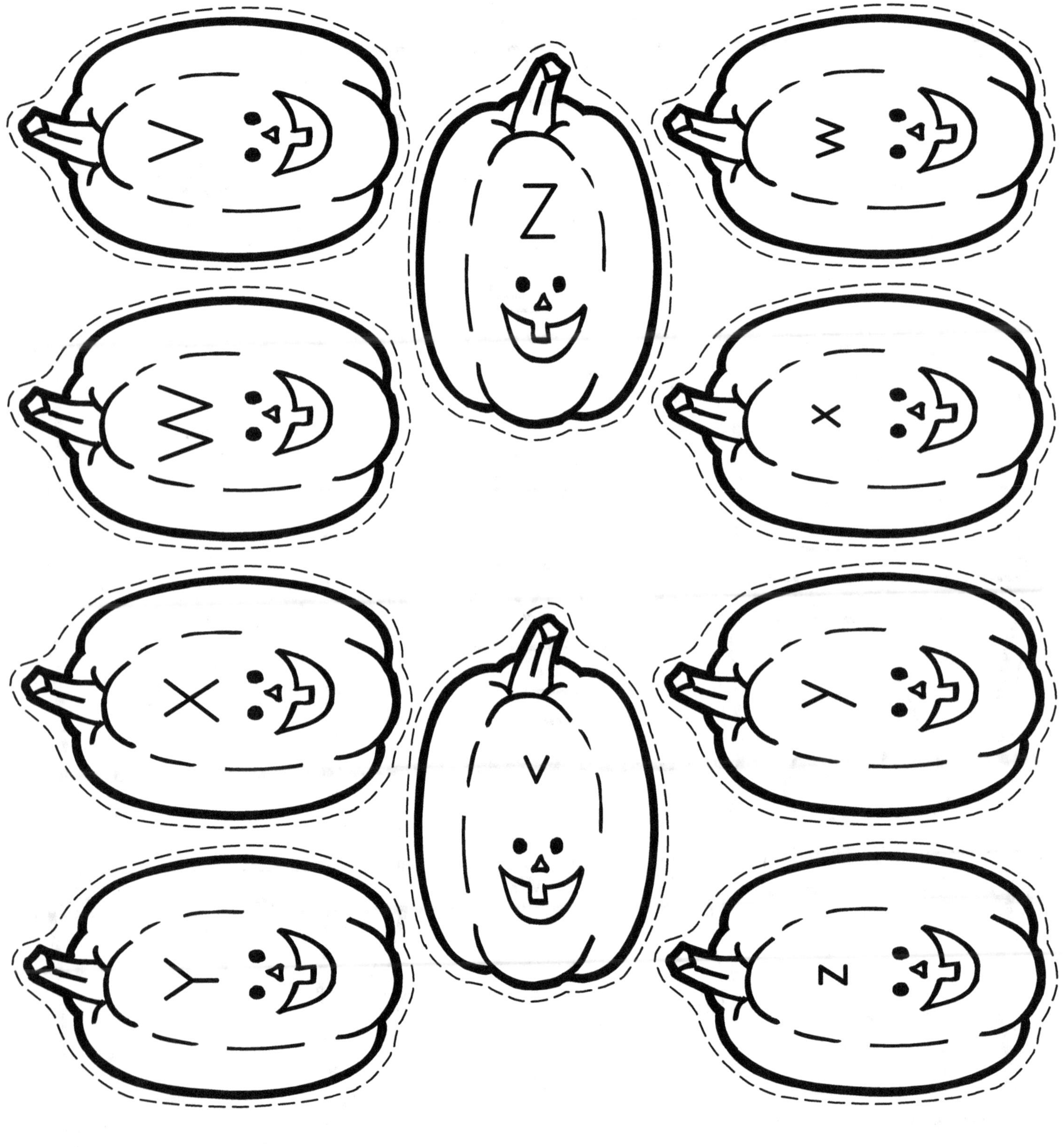

Reproduce, color, and cut out the pumpkins.

LAB20146P • 37 FOLDERGAMES FOR LETTERS • 978-1-937257-55-2 •

Fancy Socks in a Box
Recognizing Short Vowels and Short Vowel Sounds

Match Board

Assembly

Reproduce, cut out, and glue a set of oak tag handles (p. 192) to a standard-size file folder. Option: Decorate each handle with copies of the socks shown on this page. Reproduce, color, and cut out the "Fancy Socks in a Box" patterns. Glue two copies of the match board to the inside of the folder. Glue the cover art to the front of the folder. Decorate the border around the match boards, then laminate. Reproduce, color, laminate, then cut apart two sets of letter and picture socks cards. Glue an envelope to the back of the folder for game card storage. Option: Reproduce, cut out, and glue the Match Board Playing Directions to the back of the folder.

Fancy Socks in a Box Cover
Recognizing Short Vowels and Short Vowel Sounds

Match Board

Fancy Socks in a Box
Recognizing Short Vowels and Short Vowel Sounds

Match Board

Place a pair of matching picture and letter socks in each box.

Fancy Socks in a Box
Recognizing Short Vowels and Short Vowel Sounds

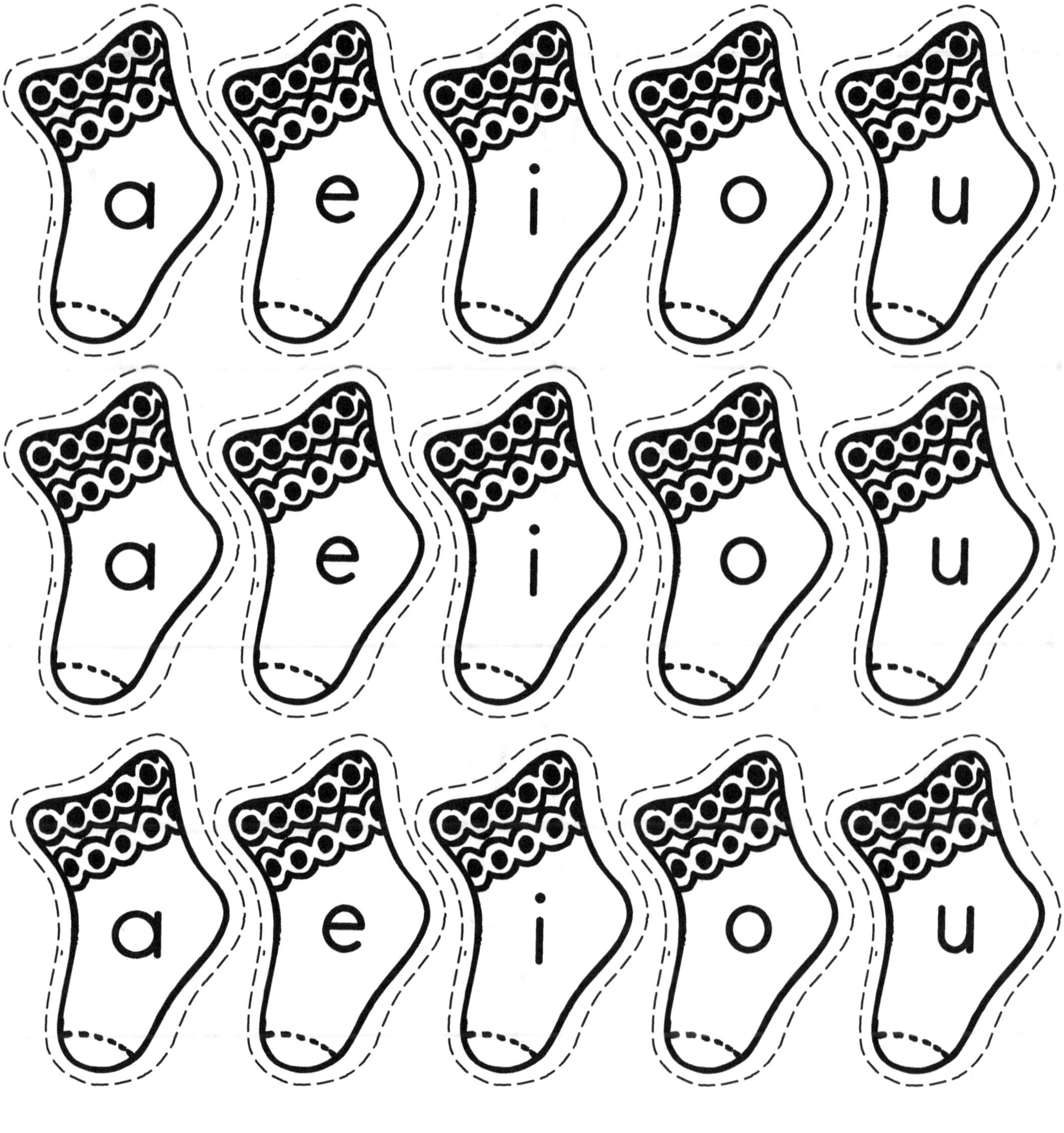

Match Board

a e i o u
a e i o u
a e i o u

Reproduce, color, and cut out, one set of letter socks.

Fancy Socks in a Box
Recognizing Short Vowels and Short Vowel Sounds

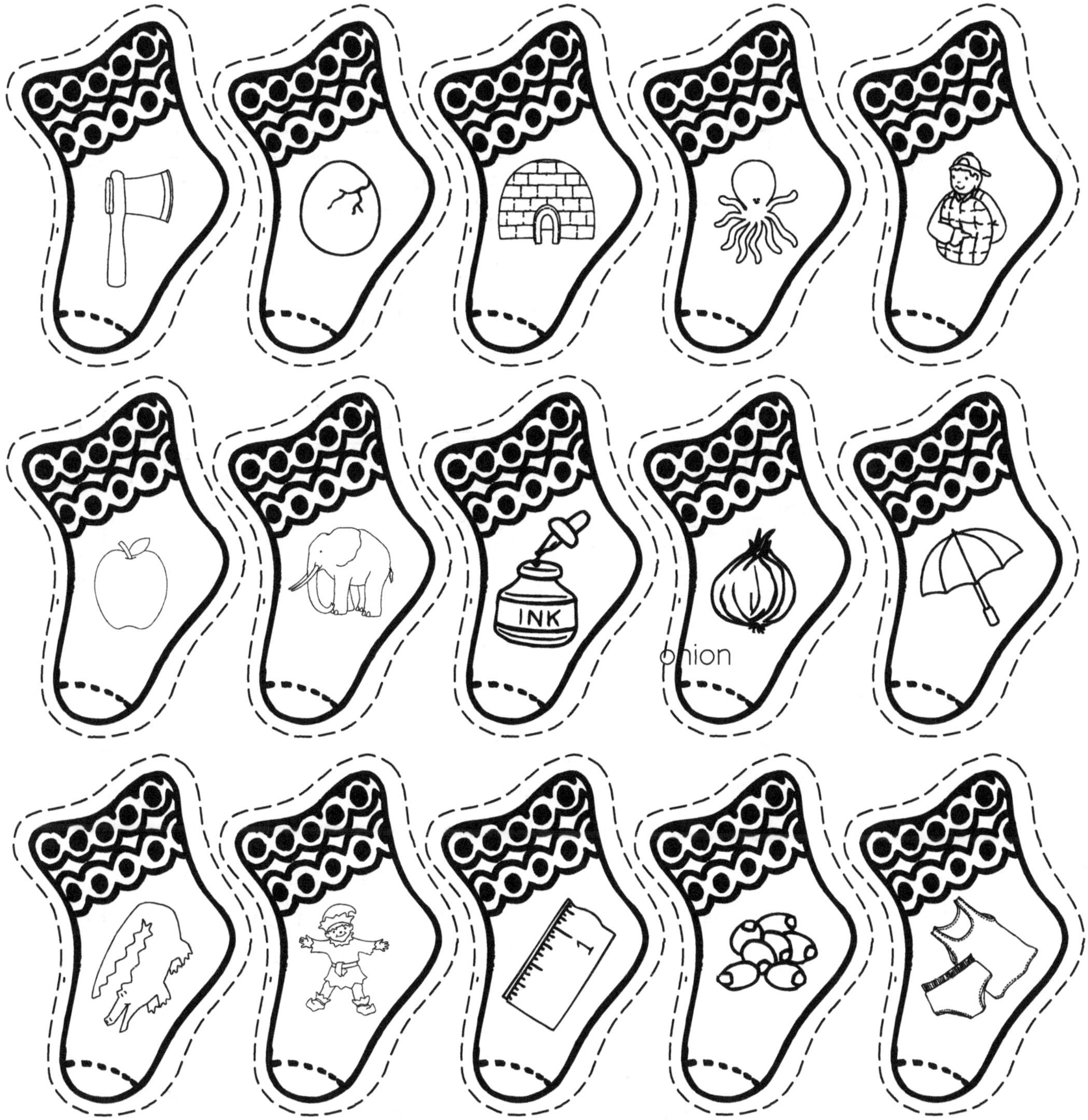

Match Board

Reproduce, color, and cut out, one set of picture socks.

Vegetable Soup
Recognizing Short Vowels and Short Vowel Sounds

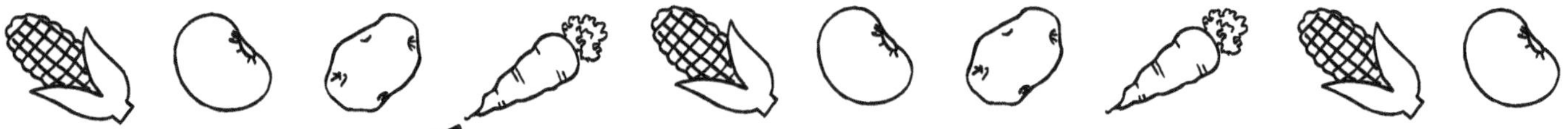

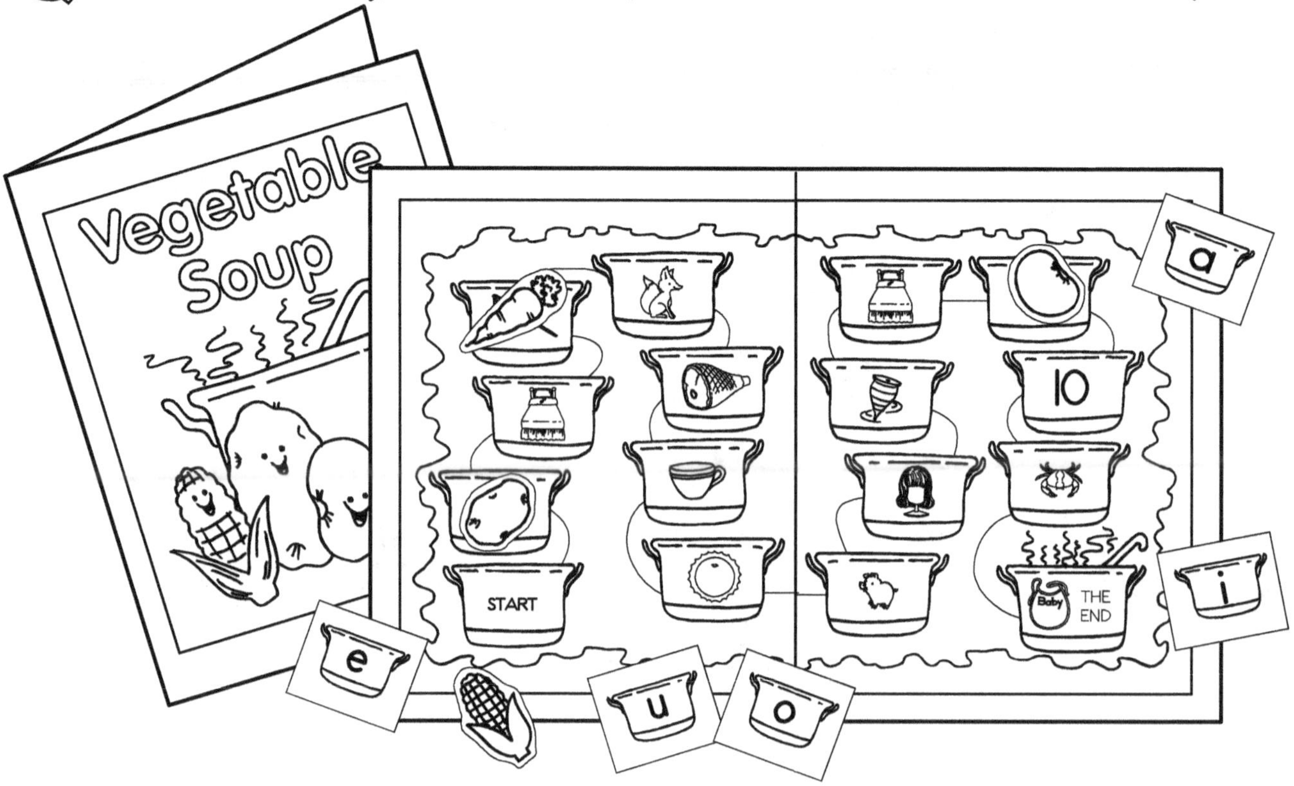

Trail Game

Assembly

Reproduce, cut out, and glue a set of oak tag handles (p. 192) to a standard-size file folder. Option: Decorate each handle with a copy of the vegetables shown above. Reproduce, color, and cut out the "Vegetable Soup" patterns. Matching in the center, glue the game board patterns to the inside of the folder. Glue the cover art to the front of the folder. Decorate the border around the game board, then laminate. Reproduce, color, laminate, then cut out the pawns and two sets of game cards. Glue an envelope to the back of the folder for pawn and game card storage. Option: Reproduce, cut out, and glue the Trail Game Playing Directions to the back of the folder.

Pawns

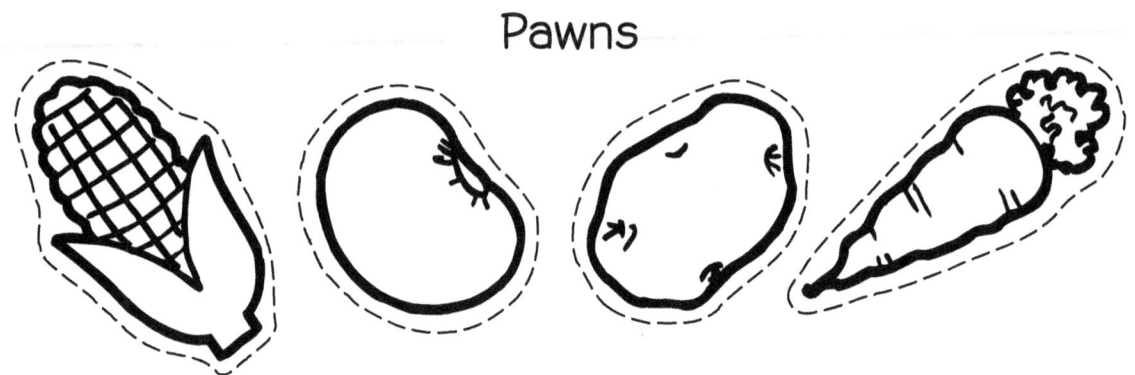

Vegetable Soup Cover
Recognizing Short Vowels and Short Vowel Sounds

Trail Game

Vegetable Soup

LAB20146P • 37 FOLDERGAMES FOR LETTERS • 978-1-937257-55-2 • © 2014 Little Acorn Books™

Vegetable Soup
Recognizing Short Vowels and Short Vowel Sounds

Trail Game

Help the vegetables find their way to the vegetable soup pot.

Vegetable Soup
Recognizing Short Vowels and Short Vowel Sounds

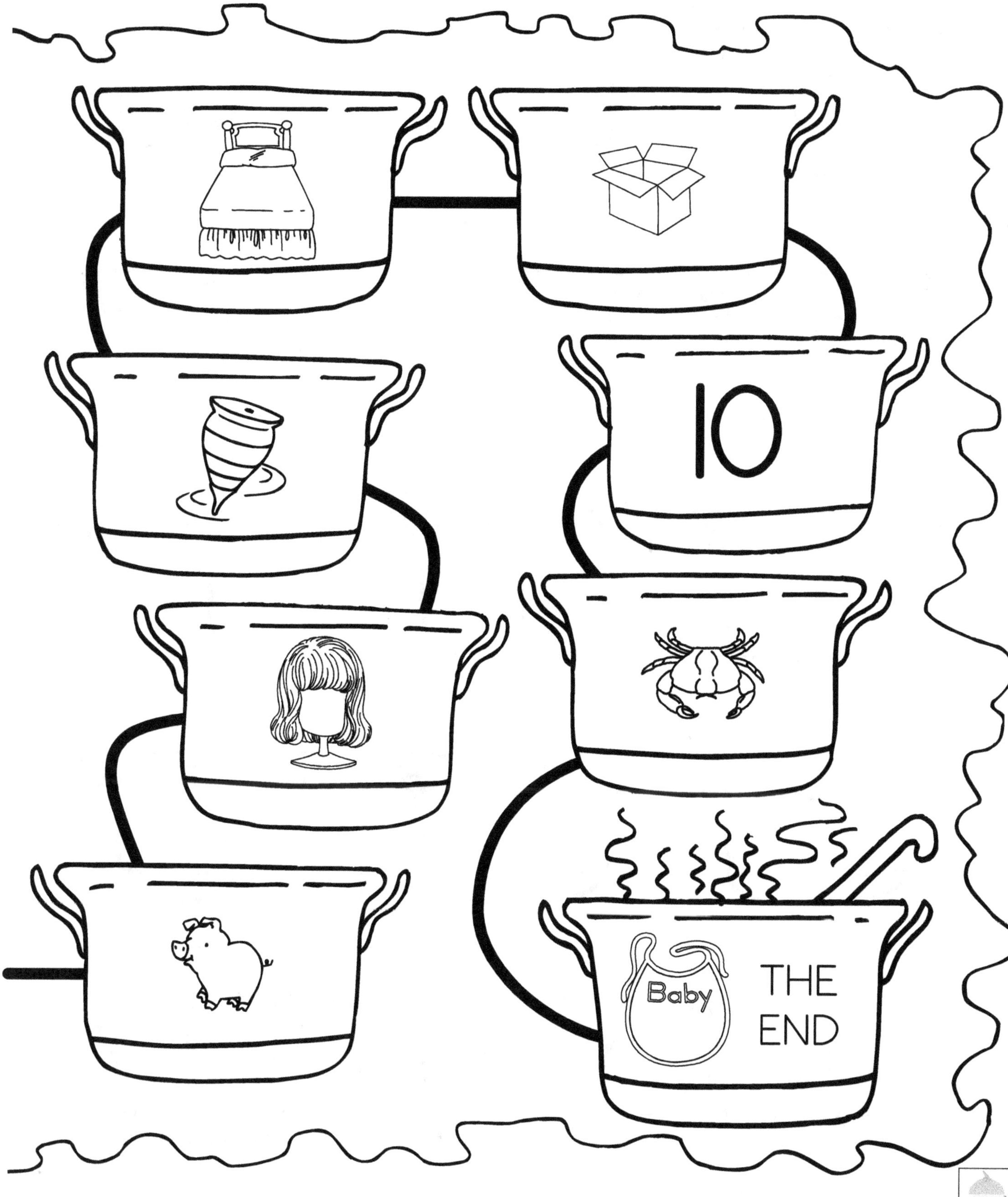

Trail Game

Vegetable Soup
Recognizing Short Vowels and Short Vowel Sounds

Trail Game

a	a	a
e	e	e
i	i	i
o	o	o
u	u	u

Reproduce, color, and cut apart two sets of cards.

Peek-a-boo Spiders

Pocket Game

Recognizing Long Vowels and Long Vowel Sounds

Assembly

Reproduce, cut out, and glue a set of oak tag handles (p. 192) to a standard-size file folder. Option: Decorate each handle with a copy of the spiders on this page. Reproduce, color, and cut out the "Peek-a-boo Spiders" patterns. Draw a giant web on the inside of the folder. Apply glue only along the bottom and side edges, then attach the web pockets to the inside of the folder. Glue the cover art to the front of the folder. Decorate the border around the game board. Glue an envelope to the back of the folder for spider storage. Option: Reproduce, cut out, and glue the Pocket Game Playing Directions to the back of the folder.

Peek-a-boo Spiders Cover
Recognizing Long Vowels and Long Vowel Sounds

Pocket Game

Peek-a-boo Spiders

Peek-a-boo Spiders
Recognizing Long Vowels and Long Vowel Sounds

Pocket Game

Reproduce, color, and cut out the web pockets and spiders.
Apply glue only along the bottom and side edges of each web pocket.
Then attach each pocket to the inside of a folder.

LAB20146P • 37 FOLDERGAMES FOR LETTERS • 978-1-937257-55-2 • © 2014 Little Acorn Books™ 185

Pocket Game

Peek-a-boo Spiders

Recognizing Long Vowels and Long Vowel Sounds

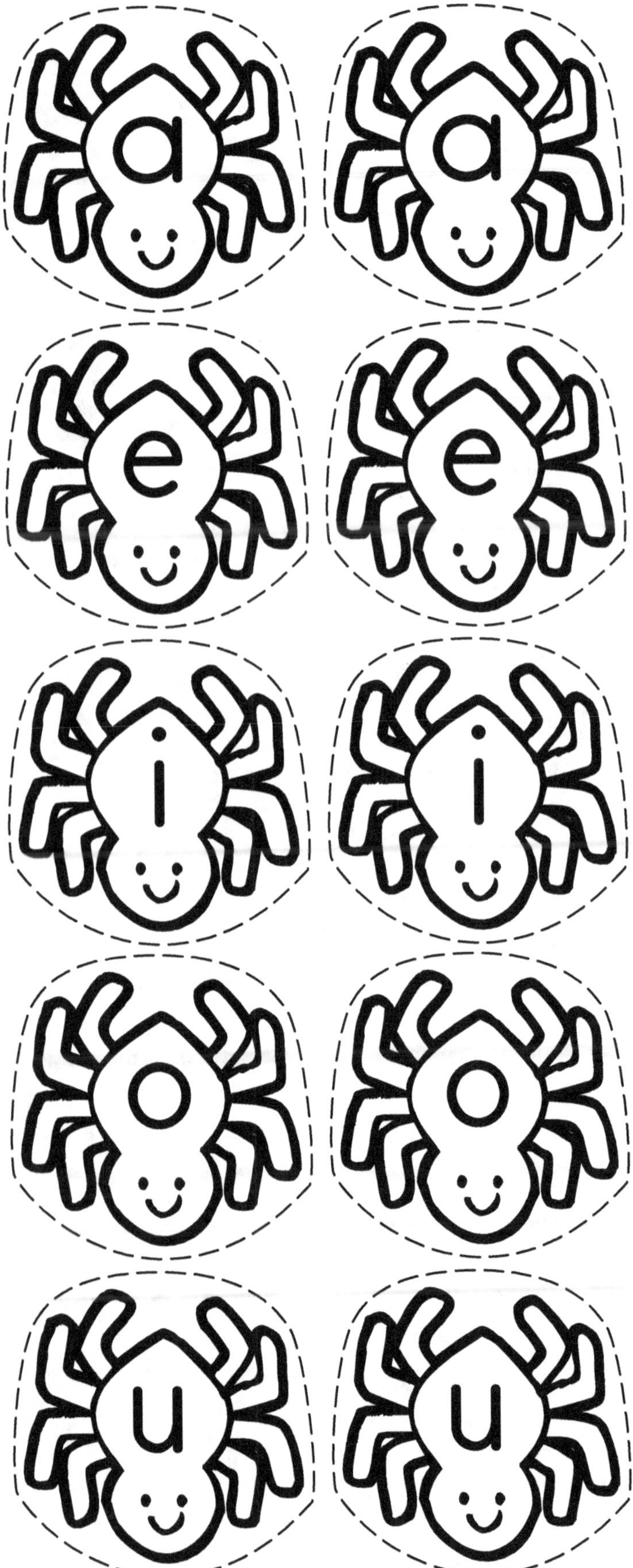

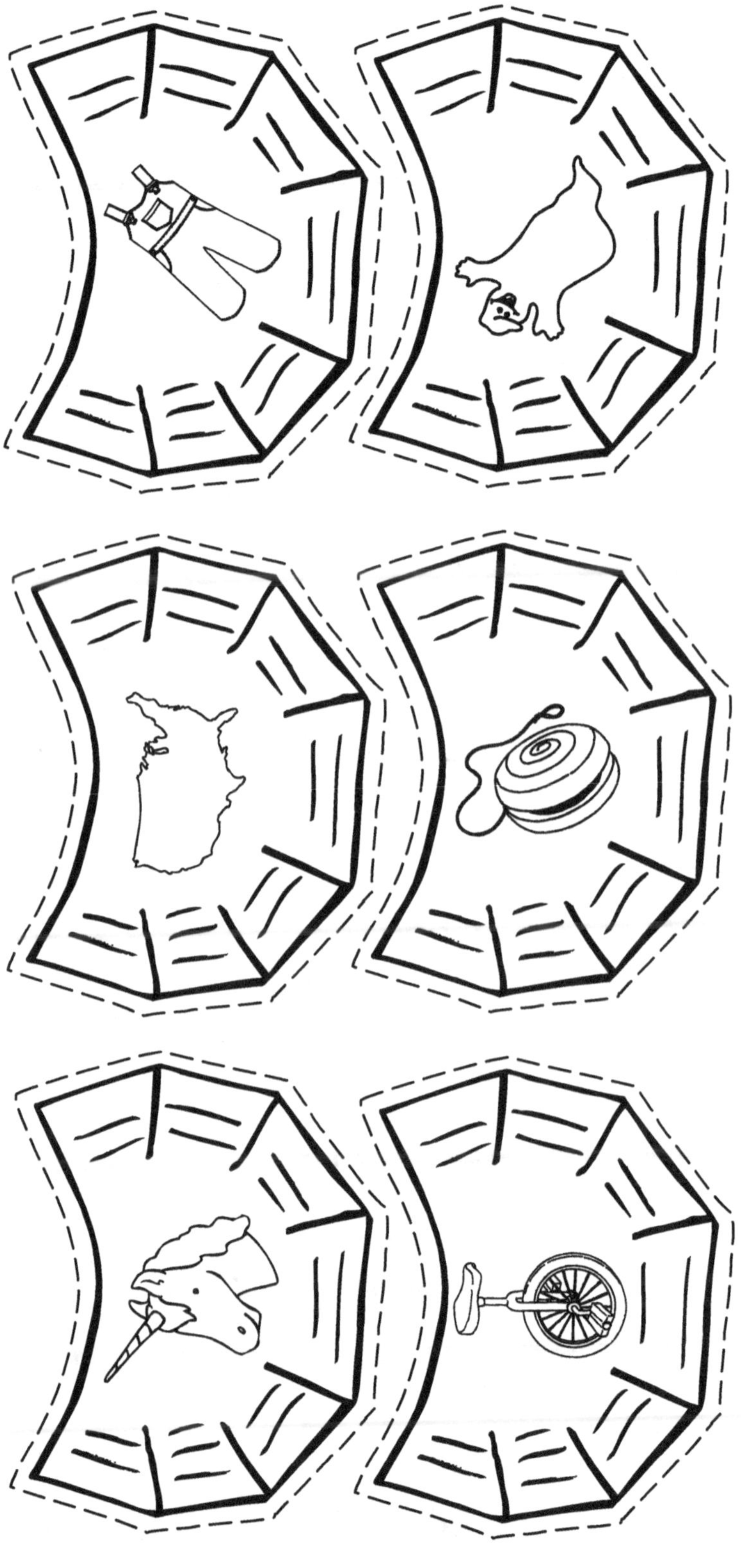

Reproduce, color, and cut out the web pockets and spiders. Apply glue only along the bottom and side edges of each web pocket. Then attach each pocket to the inside of a folder.

LAB20146P • 37 FOLDERGAMES FOR LETTERS • 978-1-937257-55-2 •

Cookies and Milk
Recognizing Long Vowels and Long Vowel Sounds

Trail Game

Assembly

Reproduce, cut out, and glue a set of oak tag handles (p. 192) to a standard-size file folder. Option: Decorate each handle with a copy of the milk containers shown above. Reproduce, color, and cut out the "Cookies and Milk" patterns. Matching in the center, glue the game board patterns to the inside of the folder. Glue the cover art to the front of the folder. Decorate the border around the game board, then laminate. Reproduce, color, laminate, then cut out the pawns and two sets of game cards. Glue an envelope to the back of the folder for pawn and game card storage. Option: Reproduce, cut out, and glue the Trail Game Playing Directions to the back of the folder.

Pawns

LAB20146P • 37 FOLDERGAMES FOR LETTERS • 978-1-937257-55-2 • © 2014 Little Acorn Books™

Trail Game

Cookies and Milk Cover
Recognizing Long Vowels and Long Vowel Sounds

Cookies and Milk
Recognizing Long Vowels and Long Vowel Sounds

Trail Game

Reproduce, color, and cut out, two sets of milk cards.

Cookies and Milk
Recognizing Long Vowels and Long Vowel Sounds

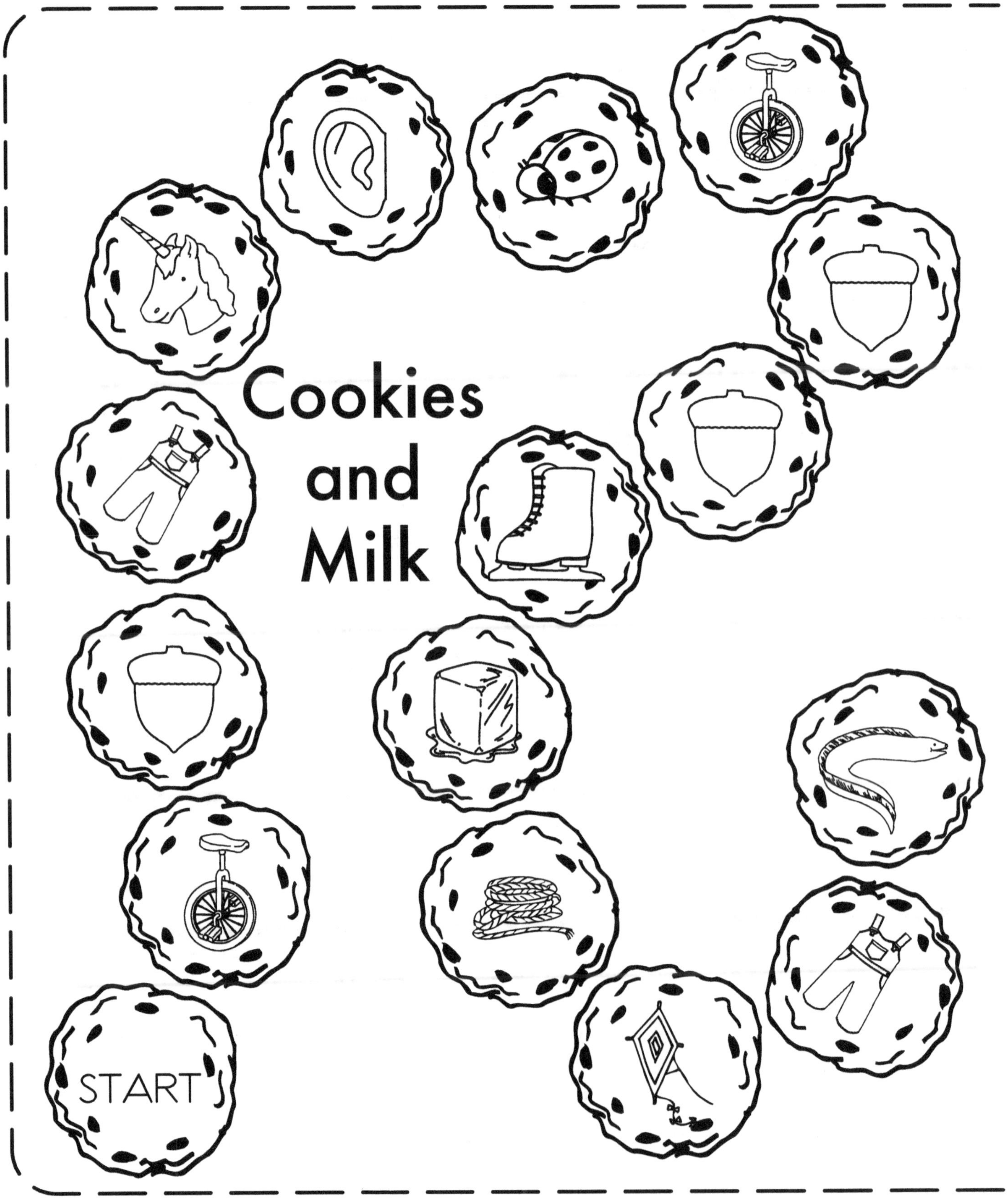

Trail Game

Cookies and Milk

Recognizing Long Vowels and Long Vowel Sounds

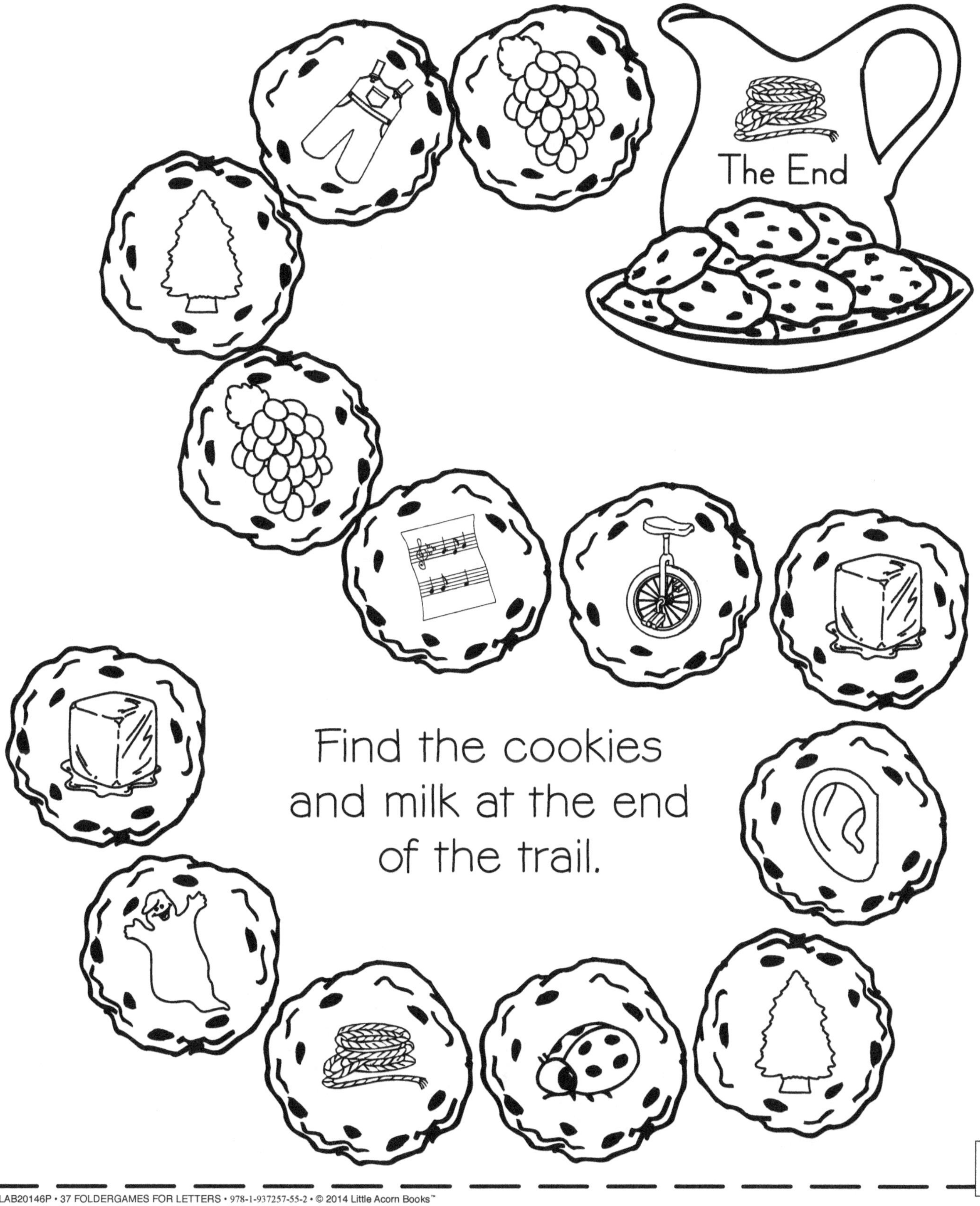

Trail Game

The End

Find the cookies and milk at the end of the trail.

Folder Handles

Reproduce, color, and cut out a set of handles for each folder game.

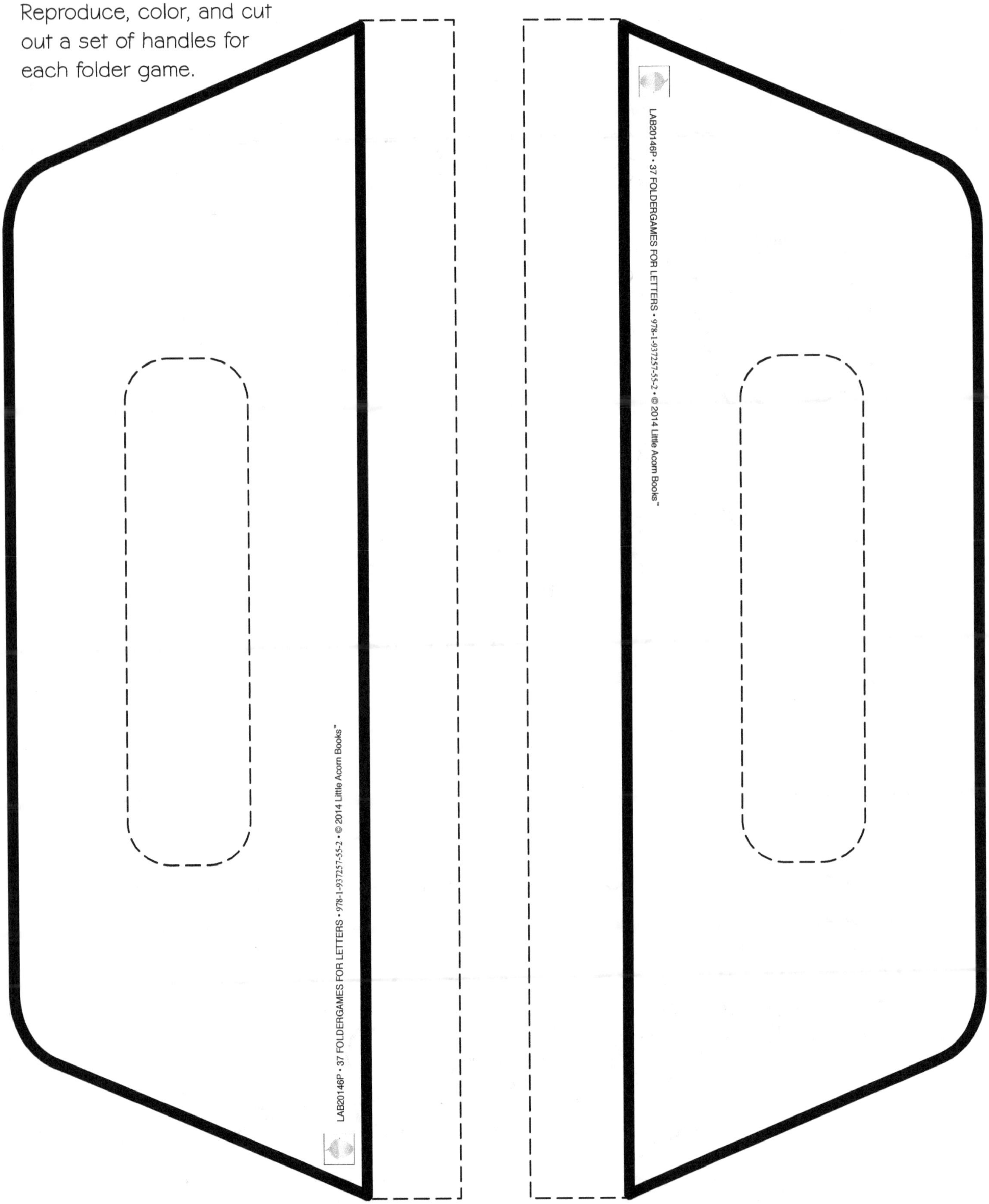

Little Acorn Books™

Promoting Early Skills for a Lifetime™

A Hands-on Picture Book Series • Infancy–Age 4

Miss Pitty Pat & Friends
Preschool–Grade 1

Mookie's Christmas Tree
For All Ages and
Not Just for Christmas

Using Crayons, Scissors, & Glue for Crafts
Preschool–Grade 1

Little Acorn Books™
Visit our web site:
www.littleacornbooks.com

www.ingramcontent.com/pod-product-compliance
Lightning Source LLC
Chambersburg PA
CBHW081456040426
42446CB00016B/3265